TIGER, TIGER

TEXT BY
Karine Lou Matignon

FOREWORD BY
Jean-Jacques Annaud

PROLOGUE BY
Boris Cyrulnik

PHOTOGRAPHS BY
David Koskas

with 131 illustrations, 108 in colour

Thames & Hudson

599 756

(2764901

Contents

PROLOGUE

The lion, yes! But the tiger? Even in the Bible, the lion was already a political metaphor: when little David, future king of the Jews, asks Saul for permission to fight the Philistines, he is deemed to be far too young. And so he describes how he killed a lion with his staff. He would never have become king if it had been a dog that he had killed, but the fact that it was a lion set him above all other men. This magnificent animal with crowning mane, mighty muscles and armoured jaws set the standard against which the value of the men that fought it could be measured.

At the opposite end of the spectrum, the knight that fled from the hare symbolized cowardice in a world where physical courage determined the hierarchy. The bee, the cow, the pig, the dog were living proof of mankind's dominion over nature. The ass, which had worked with its master since antiquity and shared his hovel, was present at the birth of Christ, and had long since entered the realms of literature for both its comic and its erotic associations, its jolly bestiality giving expression to our basest instincts.

The tiger, however, is not to be found in such folk tales – at least, not in Europe. It is nonetheless admired, just as one admires those who can kill or be killed without uttering a sound, in a form of combat that seems superhuman. Even when caged, the tiger is admired and feared. Pierced with arrows, as can be seen on Assyrian bas-reliefs, its jaws wide, ever ready to do battle even when it is dying, it demands our respect. But our admiration is also directed – perhaps even more so – to Naram-Sin, King of Akkad, who conquered the beast.

Today, such portrayals of the death of tigers are no longer acceptable. Where once the rich white man appropriated the tiger's power by killing it simply for sport, now he can only envy its lazy liberty and feel shame at having decimated the species. Of course the tiger also embodies some of our fantasies. Like the biblical serpent that represents deceit and temptation, the ass that embodies our baser elements, or the bee that symbolizes our social self, the tiger might perhaps reveal our new relationship with life. When society operated to benefit only a tiny minority – the aristocrats and the upper middle classes – women were valued for little more than their wombs, and men for their muscles. And so women were expected to follow the example of the cat – 'such a good mother' – and men looked to the fable of the pelican, which was believed to puncture its own breast in order to feed its young. The social roles of both sexes were therefore shaped by sacrifice. The woman wanted to give a child to her husband, and would sometimes pay for it with her life. And the man would seduce the woman through the strength of his arms, but would sometimes go on to lose his life in the mines, in war, or at his place of work. The purpose of their lives was to suffer and die so that someone else might live.

Today, when personal fulfilment in our culture often takes the form of adventure, we admire creatures that are free, beautiful, powerful, swift, predatory – in a word, feline. The tiger fills us with wonderment when it walks, when it attacks, or even when it sits there yawning with self-assured nonchalance, for its movements seem to give form to our own deep desires for mastery over life. Indeed the donkey no longer makes us laugh with its asinine humour, while the self-sacrificing pelican might just as well be a pigeon. As for the fertile mother who has brought eighteen children into the world, she no longer even gets a medal. But the tiger continues to fascinate and inspire us.

Let us make sure that it survives on the great battlefield of nature, so that it may continue to haunt our dreams.

Boris Cyrulnik
Psychologist and Researcher

Two Brothers: A Movie Adventure

Making a feature film is always an adventure, but when you also have the crazy idea of including dozens of tigers in the plot, the boldness of the enterprise borders on lunacy. This movie is the result of three years of hard work. Here is the behind-the-scenes story of co-operation and collaboration between a fascinated human crew and the great cats whose lives they were observing.

The ruins of a temple stand amid an ocean of leaves.

The tigress growls, lies down on the moss, stretches herself, and slowly rolls over on her side, licks a paw and waggles her behind. The mighty tiger has lost his air of arrogance and watches her, intoxicated by her powerful female scent, fascinated by the seductive movements of her body. He approaches. She gets up, simpers a little, and moves away.

She strolls along the ramparts of the temple of Angkor, the great Khmer city. Now the two tigers stand, paw each other, and embrace. The male impatiently clamps his jaws on to the nape of the female's neck, and seizes her hindquarters with his front paws. Their cries of love echo far beyond the walls of the ruined temple. 'We had to wait six months for these two tigers to fall in love, so we could shoot this scene,' explains Jean-Jacques Annaud. 'We took the set with us everywhere and looked for the signs every day. Then at last, one morning, the scene unfolded exactly as we'd hoped. You can imagine how we felt!'

A Movie Is Born

The story of *Two Brothers* is almost a personal quest for its director. His fascination with human and animal behaviour began with *Quest for Fire*, followed by *The Bear*, but it was not until 1992 that Jean-Jacques Annaud discovered the site at Angkor and heard about the Indo-Chinese tigers. The beauty of the great cats and of the Indian-inspired temples sparked the idea for a new film: two tiger cubs

Above: In *Two Brothers*, Jean-Jacques Annaud set out to film the primal emotions of love, friendship, and the will to survive.

Opposite: In the jungles of South-East Asia, several dozen trained tigers and more than two hundred technicians learned to live together during months of filming.

Everyone says the tiger is cruel.
Is it? Have you watched their eyes...
they are so gentle. He will never turn back on
his track once he decides on it, come what may.

Fateh Singh Rathore, tiger specialist

are born in the ruins of a forgotten temple. They grow up under the watchful gaze of their tigress mother and their mighty tiger father. And then one day, temple looters burst onto the scene and capture them.

It took a year to find locations in Cambodia and Thailand, and then another year of filming with more than thirty tigers, young and adult. But how would the tigers act their parts? And how could people and tigers live together in the middle of the jungle over such a long period of time? The project could never have happened without one man – one of the finest animal trainers in the world: Thierry Le Portier.

Casting a Spell

Thierry Le Portier has spent thirty-five years forging an extraordinary relationship with wild animals. His talent for communicating with tigers does not come from a mysterious pact between human and beast, but depends on a finely honed ability to watch and listen. 'The English and Americans say that when you work with animals in this way, you must continually read them to understand what's going on in their heads,' he explains. 'Careful observation and deduction allow you to anticipate and control the animal's actions.' Between the ages of one and three, the tigers were trained in the basic actions of standing still, jumping, going from one point to another, and walking and running at different speeds. 'The training is based on two principles,' he says. 'What is allowed, and what is not allowed. When I get the response I want, I reckon that material reward is useless 95 per cent of the time. The only reward should be the positive, kindly attitude of the trainer. If the animal does what I want him to do, I show him that I'm pleased: "Bravo!" Or if he doesn't, I show him: "I'm annoyed." The tiger always prefers the soothing tones.

This feeling will register much more quickly in his memory than giving him a reward of food, because if you do that, then it's his stomach that's working and not his head.'

The trick is to cast a kind of spell over the animal, and the human voice is a very effective tool for this. It intrigues the tiger, who quickly learns to understand the verbal commands associated with specific actions. While the words induce an action or an emotion, the cat also interprets the trainer's body language. However, at the moment when you least expect it, you may see the beast's true nature resurface, and this is something the trainer never forgets. 'The tiger is a predator. Nothing escapes him. Every day he tests you and watches you,' says Thierry Le Portier. 'Even after fifteen

Above: On a few rare occasions, a 'remote control' tiger took over the role of the trainer, especially if the scene looked like it might be uncomfortable for the animals.

Opposite : Throughout the filming, the trainer used his voice to instruct the tiger.

Overleaf: The trainer Thierry Le Portier rehearses with a tiger in the ruins of Angkor.

ANIMATRONICS TO THE RESCUE

When filming the tigers became too difficult or too dangerous, advanced technology was used in the form of cameras on a radio-controlled crane, or cameras operated by remote control. At other times, when the actors might have been at risk through being too close to the animals, or conversely in order to prevent the tigers, both young and old, from exposure to stress or discomfort, scenes were shot using a combination of animatronics (dummy animals controlled by electronics or cables) and the wizardry of CGI effects.

To nurse ambition in
one's heart is to carry
a tiger in one's arms.

CHINESE PROVERB

Above and opposite: These cubs, born in captivity, are discovering the joys of the jungle. As soon as they start to play, they forget that they are being filmed.

years of working with them daily, if a tiger thinks you're relinquishing your power, he'll immediately try to take control. If you want him to do something, but you don't put enough willpower and intensity into your voice because you're a bit tired that day, he'll slow things down, and if you fail to be firm enough for just one moment, the animal will – depending on his character – either stand still, go away, or attack you. The fewer mistakes you make, the quicker the animal will understand. The learning process comes from building a common language that grows richer with time. It's also a matter of developing the qualities that already exist in the animal, and playing down certain eaknesses, though never suppressing them or changing the animal's nature.'

Tigers on Set

Once the screenplay was written and a detailed storyboard was ready, the trainer was able to work out how to get the tigers to create the scenes the director wanted. The roles of the two brothers at different phases of the story had to be played by a whole team of cubs about a month and a half apart, and so the whole of Europe was scoured for pregnant tigresses. Several females duly gave birth to litters, and there was no interference in the natural birth process. Two cubs allowed the director to observe the various stages of growth during preparations for the film. There couldn't be any period of 'apprenticeship' with such young animals, but on the other hand they were naturally playful, and this made it easier to work with them. Every conceivable device was used to set up each scene. All sorts of objects – rags, packets, hooters, tin cans – were shaken about under their noses to make them take a few steps in the right direction, or to capture an expression of alertness on their little faces. Butterflies were released so that the cubs would chase after them, and tasty tidbits were attached to the end of a pole in order to get them to climb a tree or rock. The adults (the male tiger, the tigress and the old circus tiger) generally played their parts as written, but other tigers did double for them in a few scenes – just like stuntmen doubling for human stars – so that actions like jumping and running could be performed.

Each tiger had a character of its own. 'Both the cubs and the adults show a whole range of extraordinary expressions and emotions,' says Jean-Jacques Annaud. 'When the two cubs are together in the film, they are playing themselves: one is daring, while the other is quite timid.' In most families you will find one cub dominant and the other dominated.

TIGER, TIGER, BURNING BRIGHT
  IN THE FORESTS OF THE NIGHT,
  WHAT IMMORTAL HAND OR EYE
    COULD FRAME THY FEARFUL SYMMETRY?

WILLIAM BLAKE, 'THE TIGER'

Born Actors and Old Hams

'The adult tigers all have their own personalities,' says the director. 'Some are very sure of themselves, some are complainers, some are bone idle, some won't do re-shoots. Others might be more reserved, or kind-hearted, or attentive, or eager to please.' The adults had already been trained, so they were either taught specific actions that Thierry Le Portier rehearsed with them just before filming, or they would be exposed to a stimulus whose shape, movement or sound would get their attention or make them produce an expression (serious, alarmed, satisfied, happy) that would fit the requirements of the scene.

'When I'm working with tigers,' explains Jean-Jacques Annaud, 'I do what I would do with human actors: I try to construct clear situations in appropriate settings, so that I can get the responses I want. I place the animal in an atmosphere where it will spontaneously express the feelings required by the screenplay.' For example, when the two brothers have been separated for several months and then meet again in the arena, they recognize each other and refuse to fight. To film this happy reunion, two tigers that had always been together were separated on the eve of the shoot, and were then released into the arena. They expressed their delight at seeing each other again in typical tiger fashion, nuzzling and purring, and then they played together exactly as the screenplay described. The rest was a matter of editing, and the illusion would then be completed by the emotional conditioning of the viewer, in what is known as the Kuleshov effect. This Soviet cinema theorist once put together expressionless shots of an actor in three different contexts: with a half-naked woman, a bowl of soup,

and a corpse. The mere sight of these images was enough to induce spectators to read specific emotions into the actor's face: respectively lust, hunger, and sadness – although his facial expression was identical in all three sequences. This principle can naturally be applied to tigers.

Caged Humans

Angkor, the Mondolkiri region, Siem Reap, and many other areas where the film was shot had been mined – like the whole of Cambodia – first by the Khmer Rouge and then by the Vietnamese. Before filming, every site had to be inspected by landmine disposal experts. For 13 hours a day, and for months on end, tigers and

people would live and work together amid draconian security. Technicians were shut in cages or protected by netting, while the tigers roamed semi-free over several hectares of land. This ground was enclosed by a system of nets, several metres high. The film crew were told not to run or shout if confronted by a tiger, and to carry a stick designed to impress the animal, who would take it to be an extension of their hand. One scene featured a tiger racing across a large expanse of wild country in pursuit of a car. Stakes and nets were set up, with the latter fixed to poles that could be made to spring up by means of detonators if the tiger should try to escape, holding the animal back in much the same way as planes are stopped by nets when landing on an aircraft carrier.

Every morning Thierry Le Portier would go to the tiger base camp and choose those that he thought were most suited to the scenes planned for that day. 'Out of the dozen adults, we always had five or six on the set with all the cubs,' he says. Assistants were then placed at strategic points to encourage the tigers to perform the actions required. The camera team shot the film from behind their protective fencing. The tigers never worked for more than three quarters of an hour at a time. 'When it's performing, the animal can forget you completely, and so you have to keep talking to it, influencing it, and directing it with your voice. You mustn't allow it to think of anything else. If a tiger stares at an actor for more than a few seconds, I stop the scene. Perhaps nothing would happen, but the situation could also become dangerous very quickly. The animal swiftly makes the connection between its interest in the actor and my intervention, and so next time it won't look at him. You have to stay vigilant at all times – that's what keeps us safe.'

Opposite: These fire scenes were created with CGI effects, to avoid distressing the tigers.

Brothers, Gods and Enemies

The beauty and strength of the tiger are both fascinating and disturbing. It embodies the very essence of nature in the raw, in all its violence and mystery. Wherever the tiger has lived, people's beliefs have made it into an ancestor, a god, a brother. But this has never prevented it from being hunted, or captured and put on show.

Guardian of the forests and of souls bewitched

Mankind has long been fascinated by the tiger. Sometimes we have transformed it into a god, sometimes into a demon, and sometimes into a magical being or a scapegoat, perhaps in an attempt to conquer the fear that it arouses within us.

Opposite: The Tibetan deity Vajradhara, the primordial Buddha, uses a tiger as his mount, just like many other Asian gods. The animal sometimes symbolizes strength, sometimes heroism, courage or destructiveness.

From the earth, there rises a stifling heat. The tiger is in no hurry.

He ripples as he moves, and every step combines the smooth suppleness of his body with the impression of mass and weight: a velvet monster striped with darkness and light. Everything about him is ambivalent. As he follows his chosen path, he moves with self-assurance, and yet at the same time he is intently vigilant. The slightest sound alerts him. This is the early 20th century, in the heart of the Cambodian jungle. The tiger reigns supreme. He has made his lair among the ruined temples, and as he passes, his shadow caresses the moss-covered carvings. His image is sculpted into the stone. Here you can see the monks fleeing at his approach; there you see him devouring a man; further along, a line of elephants harnessed for the hunt and mounted by warriors armed with brandished spears advances on a tiger that is crouching, poised to attack.

Companion of the Gods

Today the tiger has been relegated to the margins of the old Khmer civilization, but the sculptures in the old temples vividly recall what was once a marriage between these ancient people and their tigers. Angkor was inspired by the myths of Hinduism, mixing its own culture with animist and Buddhist elements of Indian philosophy, which was and still is characterized by its reverence for animals. Here you find Garuda, a deity with the beak of an eagle, the body of a man, and the feet of a lion; Shiva the destroyer sits mounted on his sacred bull – his eyes symbolize the sun, the moon and fire all in one, and his very gaze kills the tiger, which he then skins; there are sacred serpents, allegories of fertility, demons and divine protectors. Within this pantheon, between Hanuman, the monkey king and son of the wind, and Ganesh, the god with an elephant's head, stands the tiger. Sometimes an ally, sometimes a threat, it is a sacred beast, endowed with all the powers that help the community to exorcize its suffering and to give expression to its hopes.

In the Sunderbans, a mangrove swamp on the border between Bengal and India, the villagers worship the tiger (see page 126), and if it kills a human, this is a sign that they must find ways to appease Bonobibi, goddess of the forest, and Daksin Ray, a god with a human face that sits astride a clay tiger. This cult is common to both Muslims and Hindus in the area.

Forces of Good and Evil

The Buddhist belief in reincarnation is based on a cycle of births and rebirths of the soul that may be

Above: Fascinated by their agility, invisible presence and silent gait, mankind has often attributed big cats with supernatural powers. The Aztecs saw them as 'the sun walking through the night to rejoin the dawn.'

Opposite: Secretive by nature, the tiger prefers to make its home in ruins or rocky caves, which it only leaves at nightfall – a habit that may have seemed magical in the eyes of many humans.

BEWARE OF THE TIGER
MORE THAN THE LION, AND A BAD
DONKEY MORE THAN THE TIGER.

ARABIAN PROVERB

Previous pages: The tiger's predatory nature has made such an impression on the human imagination that it has often been attributed with the power of judgment. Thus throughout Asia it has become a major symbol of justice and punishment.

Opposite: The tiger is not only an ally of the gods, but also the undisputed master and guardian of the forest.

manifested in their earthly form either as humans or as animals. Perhaps this is the source of the worship of many deities associated with animals. The mother goddess Devi, for example, symbolizes the feminine principle, and like most of the goddesses in the Hindu pantheon, she has an ambivalent nature that is both benevolent and frightening at the same time. Her name changes according to circumstances. When she is fighting against demons, she is known as Durga, and astride a tiger she quells violence and brings peace to the world. In her incarnation as a destructive force, however, she is transformed into Kali, and the tiger that accompanies her symbolizes her wrath. The tiger has also become a companion to Buddhist monks. For them it is not a symbol of waging war, but of taming the forces of nature, and so the tiger takes on the form of a large and easy-going cat. Nevertheless, in Buddhist symbolism, the tiger still has a dual nature: it may represent anger, but equally it stands for faith and the spiritual journey, while the forest in which it hides is a jungle in which every bamboo stalk represents a sin.

In China, the original birthplace of the tiger, its primary role is that of a messenger between the human world and the spirit world. Thus it was considered benevolent during

THE KINGDOM OF THE TIGER
    IS CALLED KANDANG BALOK.
        THERE THE KING OF THE TIGERS LIVES IN A HOUSE
            BUILT OF HUMAN REMAINS, WITH A ROOF
                MADE FROM THEIR BRAIDED HAIR.

MALAYAN LEGEND

the Shang dynasty (1700–1050 BC), whereas during the period that followed (the Zhou dynasty, 1050–221 BC), it was seen as a creature to be feared, an enemy that had to be confronted. However, it was also believed to possess the power to drive away evil spirits, and funerary effigies of the animal were placed inside tombs, so that the tiger could accompany the dead on their journey.

The great cat was a symbol of rebirth at the time both of Alexander the Great and of Genghis Khan. It crossed the routes of the nomads, from the Black Sea to the plains of Mongolia, and entered the art of the steppes, where its familiar shape decorated the harnesses of horses, funerary objects, and rock art. In Thailand, until the end of the 19th century, if several people were accused of committing a crime, they were made to face a tiger, and whoever was eaten first was deemed to be guilty. In Sumatra, where Islam has flourished for five centuries, the people still believe that if a tiger devours a man, it is merely obeying Allah's wish to punish him for wrongdoing.

Offerings to the Tiger God

The menace of the tiger has made an indelible mark on the minds of the Asian peoples who share or have shared their land with the great cat, and all their beliefs are filled with contradictions and ambiguities.

So it is that many have hunted it mercilessly, and yet have also built temples to worship it, or appease it, or seek its protection. Even today in Sumatra, offerings are made every day in the temple of Cheng Hoon Teng, where the rhythmic gong accompanies the prayers of the monks. As humans and tigers are both the children of Mother Nature, they are viewed in India as brothers, to the extent that among certain tribes in northern Bombay there are frescoes depicting a fraternal tiger growing up in the midst of humans. Stone altars bear offerings to Vaghadeva, the tiger god, who is guardian of the forests. Here the great cat is not regarded as an animal, but has become a hero, an idol that is able to grant all wishes, no matter how personal.

Amulets and Superstitions

Sometimes the tiger does not simply symbolize power, but its sensuality also provokes sexual desire. Even today there are places in India where phallic sculptures of the cat are used during fertility rites. These indicate that its sexual prowess can be

Opposite: Detail from a temple in Cambodia. The Indian goddess Durga embodies the duality of the tiger itself, being both benevolent and fearsome. The tiger accompanies her into battle against demons.

UNDER THE SIGN OF THE TIGER

Astrology goes back to Mesopotamian civilizations, and from Tibet to Egypt, through China, India and North America, the stars were almost all organized in systems that represented animals, either real or imaginary. Of the twelve animals that represent the years of the Chinese zodiac, the tiger is in third position. Impulsiveness and the need to take up impossible challenges are the attributes of this passionate, quick-tempered sign. The tiger is also one of the most powerful figures in Vietnamese astrology. Marco Polo was born under the sign of the tiger, as were Mohammed and Karl Marx.

The Legend of Prey Thiam Kla

A long time ago, before the age of the great kings of Angkor, the tiger was a harmless animal. A young warrior could transform himself into a tiger if he needed to, but his secret had to remain unknown to the rest of the community.

One day, the wife of one of these warriors asked her husband to hunt a doe, which he did after transforming himself into a tiger. Before he did so, he asked a friend to hit him three times with a stick when he returned from the hunt, in order to restore his human appearance.

After capturing the doe, the young warrior who had changed into a tiger followed the path to the village to find his friend and once more take on the body of a man. But when the friend saw the tiger coming, he ran away as fast as his legs could carry him.

The hunter went to see his wife, but she was afraid of him. Wherever he went, people ran away. And so he went to live in the forest, and remained a tiger forever. Alone and abandoned by his tribe, in the course of time he came to hate human beings, and began to plot his revenge. Today he still waits weeping on a rock, and kills every human being that passes within his reach. And that is how the tiger became bad.

Opposite: The Bhil, a tribal people who live in central Hindustan, believe in a hell for tigers, whereas others, like this old ascetic at prayer, prefer to honour them. In China, an emperor would sit upon a tiger skin to symbolize his power.

GOD CREATED THE CAT
IN ORDER TO REMIND IT
THAT IT WAS ONCE A TIGER.

CHINESE PROVERB

Opposite: Although the tiger is not native to Japan, it can be found in Japanese art, due to the influence of China. This sandalwood mandala, depicting a peace-loving tiger as companion to a number of sages, is also a recurrent theme in Korean art.

transferred to humans. In order to gain the protection of the goddess of marriage, couples wear shawls of red and yellow. If the deity sanctifies the marriage, they can be assured of a bright future; otherwise, the shawls may change into tigers that devour them. In China it is the couple's trousseau that bears the imprint of the tiger. It is a very real presence in the lives of the Chinese, who still believe that anyone who falls victim to it will become a spirit doomed to serve the animal for the rest of time. Wearing amulets and other accessories with a tiger motif may be a protection against disease. In the countryside around some north-eastern provinces of China, such as Shanxi, Shaanxi and Gansu, small children wear gloves, hats and bibs made by their mothers in the image of the tiger. During the festival of the dragon boats, which takes place after the first harvest of the year, the figure of the tiger decorates the hulls in order to ward off evil, and children are given tiger-shaped objects to bring them luck. In order to endow these with power, they have the Chinese letter *wang* drawn on the front, meaning 'emperor', and there are said to be similarities between Chinese script and the markings on the face of a tiger. The Chinese believe that by giving a newborn child a name associated with the cat, they will also give it every chance of enjoying the same dynamic strength.

IT IS BETTER TO HAVE LIVED FOR TWENTY-FIVE DAYS
AS A TIGER THAN FOR A THOUSAND YEARS AS A SHEEP.

TIBETAN PROVERB

There are frequent allusions to tigers in everyday life in China, particularly through proverbs, which treat the big cat with varying degrees of respect. For example, the expression 'Raising a tiger brings misfortune' denotes that happiness can lead to trouble. 'The tiger roars when the wind rises' indicates that people must take advantage of their opportunities. 'A tiger father will not produce a dog child' reassures the brave man that his progeny will inherit his own qualities. You may do yourself damage by 'haggling with a tiger over its fur', i.e. by underestimating the person you are dealing with. On the other hand, you have avoided great danger if you have 'escaped from the tiger's jaws', and taking risks is known as 'grasping the teeth of the tiger'.

Weretigers

Our ancestors were prey to the big cats, and so the fear of being eaten has remained one of our oldest and deepest nightmares. In order to overcome it, people invented stories. Folklore is rich with tales in which humans seek to identify themselves with the tiger and are transformed at night into weretigers – the Asian equivalent of the werewolves of European myth. In India, tigers that have become man-eaters have helped to foster this myth. In Malaysia, some believe that there are groups of weretigers living in human form right in the heart of the villages, and any stranger will also be suspected of such transformations.

A Malaysian folktale tells of the terrible fate of a man who came to settle on the outskirts of a village. Just a short time afterwards, a tiger attacked the cattle. The stranger was immediately regarded as the prime suspect, and so the villagers set a trap for him. The stranger came back from the forest, pursued by a tiger, and thought he would find refuge, but the following morning, the villagers were certain that they had caught their weretiger, and so they killed him. Malaysian folklore, just like many Chinese myths, contains a number of tales in which men wear striped clothing, and need only to take off their clothes in order to be transformed into tigers that kill the unwary. There is also a well-known story of a man who visits some friends, falls ill, and begins to vomit out chicken feathers; the night before, a tiger had done a great deal of damage in the hosts' henhouse. Another tale tells how a young bride, hearing her husband return at dawn, wants to surprise him, but then discovers that he has the body of a tiger. It often happens in these

Opposite: A Javanese tribal mask in the form of a tiger. By disguising themselves as tigers, men pay homage to the gods that are escorted and guided by these animals. It is sometimes a way of asking for the tiger's protection, and of appeasing its wrath, but it can also be a manifestation of human superiority by mocking the animal.

TIGER AND DRAGON

In Asian folklore and mythology, there is a fantastic bestiary in which animals are endowed with extraordinary powers. The dragon is often associated with the tiger; the former appears in the sky, while the second hides away in the bamboo forest. They both embody power over the entire animal kingdom. When the tiger appears, escaping from rain and storms by sheltering in the bamboo, it may be seen as a special symbol: the big cat, powerful though it is, can have need of something weaker than itself.

Above: To denote his status and his authority, this Dayak chief of a Borneo village is wearing a collar made from the teeth of fifteen tigers killed by his ancestors. (State of Sarawak, 1964.)

Opposite: To the people of Siberia, the tiger is the master spirit of hunting. Many legends tell of the bond between tigers and humans, who benefit from this alliance by catching a lot of game.

Malaysian legends that the blood trail of a wounded tiger will lead its hunters to the doors of a dwelling-place. When the hunters enter, they are astonished to find that the occupant has exactly the same wounds as those their spears had inflicted on the tiger. There are similar stories in Europe, in which the tigers are simply replaced by another great predator, the wolf.

Sacred Rituals

In the Hindu religion, the *Bhagavad-Gita* (holy scripture) tells a tale of a group of *Kshatriya* – the warrior caste. There was a time when these men, armed with a sabre, were sent to fight a tiger in its own domain. When they had killed the animal, it was immediately burned amid great ceremony so that its soul might directly take over a human body before it could transmigrate into another species. The *Kshatriya* of Jaipur still perform this ceremony today. Touching the animal also allows a symbolic appropriation of its magic powers. In Madhya Pradesh, a region in central India, other religious rites are performed around the bodies of dead tigers. Every part of the body is covered with flowers and spices, for every part is filled with mystic powers: the eyes restore sight, the whiskers and claws transmit strength to those who possess them, and so on.

At the beginning of the 20th century in Malaysia, it was forbidden to kill tigers unless their attacks had become completely unendurable. Those that then died in the traps were honoured with a wake, during which they would be manipulated like puppets to look as if they were still alive. Through a network of strings, their heads would move to the rhythm of the music and the dancing performed in their honour. The Malaysians also held to the ancestral animist belief that a tiger's spirit lived on after its physical death, as summed up perfectly by an ancient Malaysian proverb: 'The tiger dies, but its stripes remain'. For these people, merely uttering the word 'tiger' was considered blasphemous; 'the striped one' was the most common euphemism. Among the Moi people of Vietnam, the tiger is still referred to as 'the gentleman', while in Java it is called 'grandfather', or 'the old man of the woods'.

Many Asian people traditionally believe that they have a special relationship with the tiger. These beliefs are based on a concept of harmony with nature that, for the most part, has never been accepted in the West, where religious ideas are fundamentally based around the concept of human dominance. Such beliefs are becoming more and more rare – generally they are only found

The tiger in the tiger-pit
Is not more irritable than I.
The whipping tail is not more still
Than when I smell the enemy
Writhing in the essential blood
Or dangling from the friendly tree.

T. S. Eliot, 'Lines for an Old Man'

DO NOT BLAME GOD FOR HAVING CREATED
THE TIGER, BUT THANK HIM FOR NOT GIVING IT WINGS.

INDIAN PROVERB

among semi-nomadic hunters who perceive no division between nature and culture, and no separation of people and animals. They live in harmony with their environment, and they do not talk of possessing the land, for they belong to it. In such a context, the tiger is part of a belief system in which it is seen not as dangerous, but as a deity that demands vigilance. This is certainly the case with the Tungus of Siberia, who regard it as the guardian of the forests and mountains – the spirit of the taiga. The Udege tribal people call it 'Amba', and try to avoid killing it. If the worst should come to the worst, they hold a ceremony of mourning around the body. But they also view this as a means of warning other tigers, who must take note of the price their colleague has paid for its imprudence.

Soul-Eaters

From Korea to Malaysia, and through Siberia, the tiger is incorporated into shamanistic beliefs. In their conviction that the beast roams the forests in search of spiritual prey, the village shamans never venture forth without taking along an image of the tiger. The word 'shaman' itself derives from the Tungus word *chaman*, which actually means 'to leap'. As an intermediary between his people and the spirit world, the shaman is guided by the spirits of animals – including the tiger – that appear to him in visions. There, to

see a tiger wandering through one's dreams means something quite different from the Western psychoanalytic interpretation, which – far from interpreting the creature as a friend or guide – would make it a representation of humanity's instinctive and sexual urges.

Léon Daudet, in *L'Homme et le poison*, tells the extraordinary story of a tiger that proved itself capable of actually devouring a soul: 'A famous explorer gave himself an injection of cocaine, to see what it was like, and afterwards in the corner of his room perceived a magnificent tame tiger, for which he suddenly felt a great affection. When the intoxication passed, the beautiful animal had disappeared. "Oh well," said the explorer, "I'll find it again tomorrow." But neither the next day nor during the days that followed, no matter how much of the poison he took, did he ever see his lordly tiger again, for it had disappeared forever in the jungle of hallucination. Six months later, he killed himself for grief, or at least his cocaine-induced suicide had as its pretext the absence of the beloved tiger.'

Opposite: The Indian deity Shiva is both destroyer and creator. Lord of men and of animals, he is often depicted meditating on a tiger skin, like the ascetic in this painted manuscript of 1670.

THE TIGER IN MARTIAL ARTS

Xing Yi Quan is an ancient Chinese martial art. Its movements are based around five elements and twelve animals, including the tiger. Students are advised to emulate the tiger's attitude rather than imitate it physically. Hung Gar is a style of kung fu that is inspired by five legendary animals: the crane, the snake, the dragon, the leopard, and the tiger, which represents strength and stamina. According to legend, it was an Indian Buddhist monk, Boddhidarma, who first taught the monks of Shaolin Temple new forms of self-defence and a better way of life.

The Spirit of the Hunter

Tiger-hunting has always been considered a supreme test of prowess. In different civilizations, the hunt has played a variety of roles. To some, the tiger is a member of their clan, but to others it may be a means for men to prove themselves, turning nature into a show of strength.

Above: Pits were one of the many methods used to capture tigers.

Opposite: At the beginning of the 20th century, rich Europeans rushed into the jungles of Indo-China to kill the beast that was then considered to be the supreme trophy of big game.

There is no sign that anything bad is about to happen, and yet the tigress is disturbed.

Her cub wanders innocently ahead. The two of them are strolling through the jungle. Suddenly the tigress stops in mid-path, and sniffs the air in alarm. Still unaware of what is happening, the cub trots on a few paces. When it finally turns back, its mother has disappeared: she has fallen into a rectangular pit that had been hidden by branches. The tigress snorts and roars in her fury. She leaps up, trying in vain to climb the side of the pit. After a moment, something stirs up in the branches. The tigress pauses, then tries to leap out again. A horn sounds. From a hide overlooking the trap, a lookout has given the signal. A line of beaters, armed with tin bowls, drums and muskets advances towards the pit, and the tiger is surrounded. Next come the elephants, with hunters sitting in their howdahs, and they too form a circle round the pit. The tigress cowers at the bottom, her ears pinned back. Suddenly there is a loud explosion and a blinding flash.

Prestigious Prey

In the early 1920s, many Europeans discovered the exotic riches of South-East Asia, which was then a French protectorate. Tours were organized, and men were invited to hunt the tiger in the forests of Cambodia, Annam, or Laos, while their womenfolk visited the temples of Angkor. British VIPs in their limousines and Frenchmen in suits would mingle with colonial officials and administrators, and with missionaries, soldiers and adventurers, whose job was to organize the hunt. There were other hunters, too, in search of rare works of Khmer art that they could take away to sell in the auction rooms of London. All of them dreamed of being the pioneers of a new world tailored to suit their own needs. Their houses, symbols of colonial power, were palatial, but untamed nature was a problem for them – they wanted to be rid of its tigers. The big cat became the test of the White Hunter's courage. For the better-off, the great London coachbuilders designed vehicles specially adapted for hunting tigers at night. 'If the extinction of the tiger species seems potentially possible one day in the future – although this still appears to be a long way off,' noted a Swedish hunter named Bengt Berg in 1934, 'then it could be prevented by confining the species to residential national parks. But so long as the great cats are living in a community with natives who have no defence against them, we must slaughter the tigers without mercy; the more skilful the hunters, the better for all concerned.' And this view was nothing new. Carried away by the first accounts of these

TO HUNT THE TIGER YOU MUST FIRST
HUNT THE TIGER IN YOURSELF,
AND TO DO THAT, YOU FIRST MAKE
CERTAIN THAT THE TIGER
IS NOT HUNTING YOU.

MOCHTAR LUBIS, INDONESIAN WRITER

adventurers, at the beginning of the 19th century the West was already taking over every corner of the tiger's wild habitat, from India to China.

It had been the same in Singapore, where the British Empire had decided to set up a trading post, way back in 1819. The colonizers were full of enthusiasm, and their plantations expanded at the expense of the forests, leading to a spate of tiger attacks on the local population over the next twenty years. After that, the tiger became the object of an extermination campaign on the orders of the British rulers. Tiger-hunting was not just a favourite sport: it was seen as a public service.

How To Hunt A Tiger

It was the time of the mythical saviours from Europe, and the tiger hunt was the crowning glory of their supremacy over nature. 'During the fifteen years that I have spent in Lang Bian,' wrote the forestry inspector Fernand Millet in 1930, 'while doing my forestry work I also performed the official role of hunt organizer; I did not do this for any personal advantage, but in the interests of the government, who wished to demonstrate to foreign sportsmen the hunting resources of the game regions of Haut-Donai [now Vietnam].' The strength and the beauty of the tiger made it an ideal trophy, all the more so because it was so difficult to track down. In South-East Asia there were several

Opposite: One of the most commonly used traps to capture the tiger alive and take it to zoos was a pit covered with branches, which the animal would fall into. The same type of trap was also used to hold it captive before releasing it in readiness for an organized hunt.

WHEN A MAN WANTS TO MURDER A TIGER HE CALLS IT SPORT; WHEN THE TIGER WANTS TO MURDER HIM HE CALLS IT FEROCITY.

GEORGE BERNARD SHAW, *THE REVOLUTIONIST'S HANDBOOK*

ways of hunting it, and everyone tried to perfect his own special method. The techniques used by the natives – for instance, the Moi with their spears and crossbows – were rejected as being far too difficult and dangerous. The number of manuals and guidebooks multiplied. One of the methods most favoured by the colonial hunters was a raised hide in a tree. A rotting bait (which smells more attractive to a tiger than a live animal) would be placed at the foot of the tree, in order to lure the tiger into the hunter's line of sight. It was essential not to arouse the animal's suspicions, as generally it would circle round its prey, sniffing the air before settling down to eat. 'It's strange to see how the tiger fixes his gaze upon the hide,' noted Plas, a hunter in Indo-China. There were other methods: you could hunt with beaters and, instead of watching from a raised hide, you could observe the animal from behind a screen of branches; there was also the option of firing from an elephant's back. For centuries the great lords of India and South-East Asia hunted the tiger using their own special technique, in which nothing was left to chance. The tiger's territory was pin-pointed, and its habits studied carefully. Paths were made for it to use, and

Opposite: In Mughal India, tiger-hunting was a favourite sport. Beaters, musicians and royal standard-bearers would accompany their masters, like the Emperor Akbar, here seen hunting near Gwalior in 1580.

sand was spread on them to mark the tracks; then large-mesh nets would be stretched out over several kilometres, held up by stakes. Surrounded by lines of elephants, the tigers would then be driven into the nets by beaters (the ancient Egyptians once used the same method of driving tigers into nets). And then, beneath the gaze of the fine and noble guests up in their tiger towers, the beasts would be trampled to death by the elephants, or killed with arrows, spears, or bullets.

A Show of Power

Hunting has always been an important social event. In most groups of social mammals, it involves a hierarchy and specific rituals, notably concerning the division of the spoils. The one who kills has the power. In the early days of mankind, hunting must have given our ancestors a huge sense of power, since they could decide the destiny of the animals around them. Throwing a flint at an animal and making it run away might have revolutionized the earliest humans' way of thinking, not to mention their relationship with the beasts.

This one simple gesture was an expression of human authority and our control over our environment. Whether it was done to acquire food or to defend settlements against attack by predators, the human invention of the collective hunt (which took place about a million and a half years ago) gradually changed over the course of time into

THE TIGER'S GIFT

The Samrais are an animist people whose social life is still based around their creation myths and totems. The most important of their totems is a tree called Krovain, which is all-powerful. Legend tells that this magic tree was brought to men by the tiger, and in gratitude the Samrais warriors gave up tiger hunting. Both the tigers and the Samrais still live in the hills west of the Tonle Sap, a tributary of the Mekong.

زخاسته بود و عرق از مسام سندگان کوان شد والحضرت نجایکب یاسی و سنگ دستی

یک حمله شیر شکار انه بشمشیر اندار کار او تمام ساخت ند ربایی کسی راکه ایزد کند

کیارد که او کند داوری اکر حمله برشیرو داورد بابانش پوست برتن

WE STOOD THERE SILENTLY A FEW MINUTES IN
THE HOPE THAT SOME SOUND WOULD BETRAY
THE PRESENCE OF THE TIGER, BUT THERE WAS
THE SILENCE OF THE GRAVE.

VLADIMIR K. ARSENIEV, *DERSU THE TRAPPER*

a sport. It has fulfilled this function at least since Greco-Roman times, becoming the prerogative of warriors and aristocrats, who used it to set the seal on their authority. From India to Turkey, via South-East Asia and Mongolia, these great lords established their heroic status by hunting down the tiger. The male ego was boosted, and forests became private property, with nature becoming a theatre of power.

It was hunting that gave birth to the first nature reserves as long ago as the 7th century BC, set up by the Assyrians and Persians, as well as the Chinese and Inca civilizations. During the Chinese Shang dynasty (1700–1050 BC), tigers were reserved as prey for the kings. There are ancient texts that even describe how tigers were trained by Chinese emperors to hunt wild boar and stags. However, as well as being a royal trophy and a source of entertainment, the tiger also served an important diplomatic purpose. Not so long ago, the Indian aristocracy often negotiated the terms of a marriage according to the number of tigers included in the dowry. Besides, if you were a maharajah, there was no more delightful invitation to be had from your neighbour than to go on a tiger hunt. And if you had to entertain a visiting British dignitary, there was no finer way of forging links between the two countries. The host would naturally let the guest do the killing, simply looking on, content to play

the role of the admiring witness. A hunt of this type had to be as spectacular as possible: 'For two whole days,' wrote Bengt Berg in the 1930s, 'the jungle was an infernal row. Troops of men, armed with rifles, spades and axes, covered all the paths… With a sound like thunder, they rolled heavy blocks of stone down from the tops of hills. They set fire to the dry grass all around the dense forest and the valleys. The flames… devoured every species of animal that was unable to flee. The elephants… were trumpeting loudly.'

Spirits and Superstitions

Hunts of this kind, which were originally linked to colonialism, survived through the periods that followed, and even continued after countries had gained their independence, taking the form of safaris organized exclusively for the

Above: In the mountains of Vietnam, arrows poisoned with curare are still prepared by the Moi medicine men, in the same way as in 1925. A single drop is enough to paralyse a tiger.

Opposite, above: Big-game hunting required the help of many trackers, who would flush out the tigers at the risk of their own lives.

Opposite, below: Hunting on the back of an elephant was one of the methods most favoured by the maharajahs and their British guests.

Overleaf: Returning from
a hunt in Indo-China during
the 1920s.

Opposite: One method of
hunting involved stretching
a huge net over several
kilometres around a tiger's
territory, so that it would
be trapped, and then
captured or killed.

Below: Engraving of a tiger
hunt by Alphonse de Neuville,
1875. Improvements in the
design of guns and cartridges
in around 1870 revolutionized
tiger-hunting by increasing
the range to as much as
800 metres (875 yards).

privileged few. They were aided by guides and professional hunters from the West, whose concepts of nature and tiger-hunting often clashed with the beliefs of the local people. In the Annam regions of Indo-China, the Moi people shocked many an Englishman: 'We had just killed our third tiger in four days,' wrote the guide Fernand Millet, 'when a delegation of natives from the group that was accompanying us came to see us, and asked us to leave the rest of the tigers of the region in peace. ...And so in the lands of the tiger, it should not be thought that the natives take pleasure in seeing the hunters getting rid of these wild animals, which overrun some areas. The Moi are a superstitious people; the tiger fills them with dread, and they are convinced that there will be reprisals from wounded animals, or that the relatives of those beasts who have succumbed to the hunter's bullets will want revenge on the native people that accompanied the white man on the hunt. It is only when a tiger has carried off buffalo or pigs from a village that the Moi will set traps themselves.'

Towards the end of the 1940s, Lieutenant Colonel Arthur Locke, an administrator in the States of Malaya, was given the task of protecting the local people against all threats to security, such as Communist terrorists and tigers, both of which had overrun the jungle. He was astonished to find that the Malay people (who hunted tigers with traps, guns or nooses) hated to utter the word *harimau* [tiger] for fear that the sleeping animal might hear them. If they came across the tracks of a tiger in the forest, they would cover them with leaves as a sign of their respect, and if a tiger was killed, they would gather together to sing and to draw up a truce with the soul of the cat. 'Ask your Malay why a tiger attacks his human victims from the behind,' he wrote, 'and he will tell you that this is inevitable, because on the forehead of every person is inscribed a verse from the Koran proclaiming man's superiority over other creatures. It is this inscription that the tiger cannot face.... Many Malays also place great faith in reciting certain passages from the Koran before they enter the jungle, holding that this practice will prevent a tiger from attacking them.'

The Tiger as a Bride

Totemic animals, which are the ancestors that protect a clan, link tribal people to particular species.

Have you forgotten that night on the river bank when the tiger kissed me on the cheek, *Tuan*? He could have killed me easily had he wished. He did not do so. I am friendly with tigers and do not care to gaze upon them when they are dead. I would prefer not to help anybody to kill one.

Sergeant Jusoh, from Arthur Locke, *The Tigers of Trengganu*

THE TIGER IS NO COWARD, IT IS SIMPLY CAUTIOUS AND
ENDOWED WITH A MARVELLOUS INSTINCT THAT WARNS IT
OF ANY DANGER; IT SENSES THE DANGER EVEN WITHOUT
SEEING THE DIRECT CAUSE OF IT, AND THAT IS WHAT
MAKES THE HUNT RELATIVELY DIFFICULT.

A.PLAS, HUNTER IN INDO-CHINA

Above: From India through Malaysia to Siberia, the soul of a tiger that has been killed on its own territory is considered to be as dangerous as the live animal, because it is capable of devouring the hunter's soul.

Opposite: Very popular among Europeans, the raised hide enabled the hunter to see the tiger coming and to take aim without being seen. A live animal or a carcass served as bait.

The slaughter of animals is limited or controlled by a number of alimentary taboos or rites. It is forbidden, for instance, to kill or eat a totemic animal, which would be tantamount to committing fratricide. This world view has brought a smile to the face of many a foreign hunter, particularly when applied to the tiger.

A tiger hunt may also be a metaphor for courtship, as it is in Siberian shamanism. At the centre of each clan is the shaman, who is the intermediary between the world of men and that of the spirits, and is a combination of oracle, medicine man, and hunting guide. According to Roberte Hamayon, an expert on shamanic practices, 'these people

only conceive of the hunt in terms of an exchange – an agreement made with the spirits of the animals. Everything depends on the art of negotiating an alliance. The term "kill" is never used. They say that the animal gives itself for love.'

Laurence Delaby, a specialist in Siberian shamanism, writes that in the early 20th century, in the far east of Siberia, the Tungus knew that there were three groups competing for hunting grounds: men, tigers, and bears. 'Each group occupies its own valley and does not allow the others to settle there. And so when a Tungus travels, he must know which animal occupies the area that he wishes to cross, so that he will not disturb it, just as he would do with other ethnic groups.' For the Tungus and the Ghiliaks, in the Amur Basin, bears and tigers are the only animals with which man has both hostile and friendly relations, as he does with other tribes. Alliances between man and tiger are common and follow similar rules to those that apply to intertribal marriages, with the dowry as a key element.

Marriage rites between humans and animal spirits are a recurring theme in these tribal groups. Delaby writes: 'The people of eastern Siberia believe that in daily life a female bear or tigress may fall in love with a hunter, and vice versa. Women who give birth to twins are also suspected

A Tale from Ancient China

South of the State of Chu, there lived a hunter who had a bamboo flute on which he could imitate all sorts of animal cries. Armed with a bow, he went up into the mountains and imitated the call of the stag. Believing that they would find one of their brothers, the stags arrived and the hunter killed them with flaming arrows.

One day, hearing him imitate the call of the stag, a wolf came running. The hunter took fright and uttered the roar of a tiger. The wolf ran away, but then a tiger appeared. Terrified, the man imitated the growl of a large bear. The tiger ran away, but believing that it would meet one of its fellows, an enormous bear now arrived.

When it found nothing but a man, it hurled itself at him, tore him to pieces and ate him. And even today, those who use tricks instead of relying on their own abilities will always meet a similar fate to that of the hunter Feng Xuefeng.

Opposite: In addition to being an entertainment, hunting also had a social function. By killing the master of the forests, the aristocracy showed off its power, as in this royal hunt, where the idea was to prove one's valour by killing as many tigers as possible

HUMAN BEINGS DIDN'T EVOLVE BRAINS
IN ORDER TO LIE AROUND ON LAKES.
KILLING'S THE FIRST THING WE LEARNED.
AND A GOOD THING WE DID, OR WE'D BE
DEAD, AND THE TIGERS WOULD OWN THE EARTH.

ORSON SCOTT CARD, *ENDER'S GAME*

of having a bear or a tiger as a lover. The tiger gives a gift to the clan of the woman he marries as a kind of ransom paid retrospectively, whereas the man who marries a tigress offers his tribute in advance. Offerings are made at funerals, particular when the deaths have been caused by tigers.' For in order to marry a tiger, it is first necessary to die!

Funeral Rites

The main causes of war between human clans are murder and abduction. These hostile relations are also found between humans and tigers, and they are very clearly defined. If a tiger kills a Ghiliak man, the clan of this man and that of his wife go in search of the tiger and kill it. The senior member of the clan then makes a speech in honour of the tiger: 'Now we are even: you have killed one of us, we have killed one of you, and so now we shall live in peace. Do not attack us again, for if you return, we shall kill you.' The funeral rites are similar to those of the big cat: after lighting a great fire next to a cage in which lie the remains of the hunter and the tiger, the members of the clan sit facing one another and throw pieces of tiger meat across the fire. If a Golde (a Tungus from the Amur Basin) happens to come across the tracks of a tiger, he throws his rifle down and bows: 'Ancient one, give us the chance to hunt. Give us game, send us something to eat.' It is considered wrong to hunt an animal that is

already being pursued by a tiger. If a hunter should accidentally kill such an animal, he will touch neither its fur nor its flesh, and he will murmur to the tiger: 'It is not I who have killed it, but you.'

Talking With Tigers

In 1902, Vladimir K. Arseniev, an officer of the Tsar, was exploring the impenetrable Ussuri Land region, on the border between Siberia and China. He met an indigenous trapper from the Tungus people, Dersu Uzala, who became his guide and friend. Through his work as a hunter in the taiga, he knew all that there was to know about tigers, having also fallen victim to one in his youth. He feared and respected them, and in the manner of the Udege people, he called them 'Amba'. Sadly, his love for them, like the shamanic rites, proved powerless to prevent the intensive hunting that typified that period. Hunting was regarded as a sport, and was freely practised, first by the army officers and then by the high-ups in the Communist Party. Dersu Uzala, meanwhile, continued to talk to the tigers. He could read their territory and their tracks, and tell where they had passed, and

Opposite: Big-game hunting contributed to the myth of European superiority. These three officers have returned from a hunt in Deccan, India, and are showing off their trophies as proof of their conquest of Nature. The two surviving cubs would be sold to a zoo or circus.

OFFERINGS AND VODKA

Any Golde (the tribal people of the Amur basin) who kills a tiger is in torment if the spirit of the animal should appear to him in a dream. This is a sign that he must pay a ransom. Speakers are then summoned – one for the hunter, and one for the tiger, the latter sometimes being a member of the Aktenta clan (the name means 'born of the tiger'). The ransom – a silk scarf, a pot, some vodka, pieces of meat, and some fish – will then be hung up in the bushes for the spirits to claim.

Previous pages:
Transporting a tiger killed at
Djiring, Indo-China in 1934.
Colonial hunters frequently
came up against the
superstitions of the local
people – beliefs that were
reported in many guidebooks.

Opposite: A hunter from
Tonkin, Indo-China, 1907.
During the 1980s, a
programme called 'Arms for
Food' made many hunters,
peasants and ex-soldiers in
the region surrender their
guns. However, hunting with
crossbows has continued.

he knew that the hunted tiger almost always finished up reversing the roles and tracking his pursuer.

'Why are you following us?' he would ask. 'What do you want, Amba? We are walking along the path, and are not disturbing you. What good will it do you to pursue us?' One day, when he stood face to face with a roaring tiger, he cried: 'Why are you shouting at me, Amba? I am not touching you. What are you so angry about?' The tiger growled with renewed fury. 'All right, if you won't stop, I will fire and it won't be my fault.' When he raised his gun and took aim, the tiger's rage subsided; it backed away, and finally disappeared into the undergrowth. Nevertheless, Dersu had fired at it, and from that day on, he feared the angry spirit of the tiger more than he had feared its living presence.

A Fatal Fascination

'Sometimes the arrival of the tiger is announced by a little crackle of dry leaves that you can barely hear,' wrote Plas, a hunter who worked in South-East Asia. 'At other times, the hunter is alerted by a sort of mewing from the animal... The excitement is intense... There is nothing more beautiful or impressive than the arrival of the tiger – it is worth even more than the trophy itself... It is a noble animal that carries itself superbly, with a proud and imposing gait... It combines both strength and beauty – it is the king of the forest.'

This testimony is not unusual, so profound is the fascination the tiger exerts over the hunters who have spent their lives tracking it. Perhaps one of the most famous was the railway engineer Jim Corbett, who regarded the tiger as 'a large-hearted gentleman'. But this respect and admiration did not stop him from devoting his life to tracking and killing the man-eaters of northern India. He was around thirty years old when he began his career by killing the famous tigress of Champawat, which had been responsible for the deaths of 436 people. Thirty years later, he ended his mission, having 'sacrificed' another female, which he had lured by imitating the cry of the male. Here the relationship between man and beast went far beyond that of the hunter killing an animal that was judged to be dangerous or would make an impressive trophy for a collection. What Corbett did implied a much deeper belief, similar to those found among ancient peoples: the notion that in order to understand one's prey, one must envisage it from inside, and identify with it. The hunt becomes a duel between hunters, and awakens the animal side of human nature, giving a fascinating insight into a creature different from oneself.

In 1938, Nikolai Baikov described this magical process : 'The spell that tigers cast over certain Asian peoples sometimes overtakes European immigrants as well; some hunters in pursuit of big game have paid with their lives for confronting this carnivore, for they were incapable of raising their guns to fire at it. The hypnotically piercing gaze of this cruel and savage beast, totally aware of its own invincible strength, takes away the will, frays the nerves and saps the morale of the man, striking his nervous centres with inertia; the result is an instant shock to these centres, or a paralysis of the motor neurons. In this state, the man becomes an easy prey for the tiger.'

I dance on the hide of Shere Khan, but my heart is very heavy…These two things fight together in me as the snakes fight in the spring. The water comes out of my eyes; yet I laugh while it falls. Why?…My heart is heavy with the things that I do not understand.

Rudyard Kipling, *The Jungle Book*

Tigers on display

The power and ferocity of the big cats has long been considered a source of entertainment. In ancient Rome, tigers were put on show in amphitheatres. In the 18th century, on the borders of Siam, they were made to fight elephants in private arenas. The modern circus was born in 18th-century England, bringing these spectacles to the masses.

Opposite: In the early 20th century, many circuses assembled impressive collections of beasts, and the number of wild animals on public display increased rapidly.

There is a buzz of excitement in the gardens of His Excellency's palace.

Flagpoles line the avenues, hung with heraldic pennants that tell of human grandeur. An arena has been built and now awaits the tigers that are to fight in it. Below ground, a great cat paces up and down in his steel prison. Around his neck is a diamond-encrusted collar. Beneath his velvet fur, the taut muscles betray his impatience, and he growls menacingly. He senses the noisy excitement of the crowd above, and he knows that the fight is about to begin. The great ruler is in his royal seat, a gong has sounded, and the spectacle can start. In the tunnel that leads to the arena, the tiger shakes with tension, pawing the ground and snorting. At last, the heavy iron grille is raised; he leaps out, and the crowd goes wild. He takes three paces, and everyone is fascinated, thrilled, riveted. He surveys the scene, tail erect, wary but confident, and when he has finished his inspection, he takes up his position in line with the tunnel. He knows that soon his adversary will appear. Then he crouches, muscles tense, ready to fight. High on the terraces, men project their own violence onto his.

Massacre of the Big Cats

Twenty-five centuries earlier, catfights and dogfights were already taking place in ancient Greece, as we know from many sculptures. But it was the circus games in the arenas of Rome that were the most striking examples of this sporting ritual. According to Gustave Loisel's *Histoire des ménageries*, it was in 273 BC that the Senate first ordered a *venatio*, a massacre of animals with javelins and arrows to entertain the people of Rome. The sport of animal combat then spread throughout Italy, and gave rise to many spectacular events. Any occasion could be a pretext for a show: a coronation, a birthday, a military victory or a new alliance. Although these shows would vary in content, they were all designed to reinforce the power of the Emperor, to please the gods, and to keep the mob happy. The games were planned many months in advance and required the capture of thousands of animals from Africa, Asia and Europe. Half of these would perish on the way. Huge expeditions had to be organized, lasting several months and involving long journeys across land and sea. Both specialist hunters and ordinary peasants were employed to trap the animals throughout the Empire. In Persia and elsewhere, tigers were caught in nets or in pits hidden by branches.

On the day before the games, a layer of sawdust or, in Nero's time,

Above: For centuries young captive tigers were trained to fight or to become pets. The cruel practice of removing claws and teeth from pet tigers has existed since Roman times, but even today, some zoos in Thailand still declaw their tigers for public displays.

Opposite: Throughout history, fights between wild beasts have reinforced the authority of those in power. For the public, the spectacle of fighting animals was a vicarious expression of their own violent nature.

OH, THE TIGER WILL LOVE YOU.
THERE IS NO LOVE SINCERER
THAN THE LOVE OF FOOD.

GEORGE BERNARD SHAW, *Man and Superman*

gold dust, was spread over the arena, the fountains were filled with perfumed water, and aromatic herbs and spices scented the air. At dawn, there would be a procession of the animals around the arena, and the public would gaze in wonderment at the rarest of creatures and the wildest of cats. The animals were bejewelled, armoured, painted or shorn. Loud music and the cheers of the crowd would accompany these spectacles right through to nightfall, and they would go on sometimes for days or even weeks on end. The price was paid by both man and beast. In AD 80, Titus built the Colosseum, the mightiest amphitheatre of ancient times, but it cost the lives of 9,000 animals and just as many men. In AD 218, fifty-one tigers were killed to celebrate the marriage of the tyrannical emperor Elagabalus (who incidentally owned a team of tigers), and this was followed by the throats of a hundred lions being cut; the roars of rage and agony, we are told, were like the rumbling of thunder.

Gladiators, Archers and Beast-Fighters

The *venatio* took place in the heart of vast arenas that could hold up to 300,000 spectators. The aim of the hunters, who were called *sagittarii* or archers, was to kill the lions and tigers with their arrows. Some professional fighters – *bestiarii* or beast-fighters – would even enter the arena of their own free will. In AD 249, to celebrate the thousandth anniversary of the founding of

Previous pages: In Asia during the 19th and 20th centuries, royal menageries served as an entertainment for the princes and their court. The first Asian zoo to include tigers is believed to have been built by the Emperor Wu Wang in around 1000 BC.

Opposite: The modern circus was invented in England during the 18th century.

THE *BESTIARIUS* WOULD CHOKE THE LIONS
AND TIGERS BY PUSHING HIS FIST
DEEP DOWN INTO THE BEAST'S THROAT
AND GRIPPING THE BASE OF THE TONGUE.

GUSTAVE LOISEL, *HISTOIRE DES MÉNAGERIES*

Rome, a thousand gladiators dressed in gold put to death hundreds of wild animals, including ten tigers. Equally popular were fights between animals, with tigers being pitted against other powerful beasts: lions, bears, elephants and bulls. The fight masters would throw burning brands at them, or tie the animals to one another before driving them out into the arena with whips and pikes.

Condemned prisoners and slaves were also exposed to lions and tigers: they were tied to stakes, suspended in mid air, or trapped in nets, and then the iron grilles were raised to let the big cats out of their cages. Many writers have described the carnage as the tigers ran or stalked towards their victims, tore them apart or dragged them round the arena before eating them in front of the jubilant mob. Nearly every Roman menagerie in the reign of virtually every emperor boasted of big cats that were fed on the flesh of criminals. Plutarch tells the following story: 'A tiger had been given a young goat, but for two days he would not eat or touch it; on the third day, being extremely hungry, he demanded more food with such violence that he broke open the cage in which he was kept: he had no desire to partake of the kid.'

Violence in the Arena

The circus games helped to bring about the swift extinction of many species of animals – particularly the big cats – even before this form of

spectacle was abolished in AD 526. It was banned not because of its cruelty, but because of the violence that kept breaking out among the spectators! Other contributory factors, however, were the dwindling wealth of the country, the influence of Christianity, and of course the increasing difficulty of obtaining animals. But despite what was happening in Rome, tiger-killing in the amphitheatres of the Middle East continued right up to the beginning of the 12th century. Gradually the spectacle of mass slaughter came to be replaced by single combat between animals. These battles found favour with the great lords of Burma and India, and with the kings of Java and Siam, where tigers were made to fight *bantengs* – wild bulls that weighed up to 900 kg (2,000 lbs). In 1736 a tiger fought three elephants belonging to the King of Siam in the presence of a French priest, Father Trachard. 'A high bamboo fence had been erected, about 100 paces square, and in the middle of this enclosure were the three elephants. They were each wearing a kind of breastplate, which extended into a mask that

Opposite: These 19th-century engravings depict two methods of training. One was known as *en ferocité* and involved simulated combat and subjugation of the animal. The second was known as 'soft dressage', and involved the tamer and the animal coming into close physical contact with one another.

A RISKY BUSINESS

On 3 October 2003, the magician and animal trainer Roy Horn was mauled by a seven-year-old white Bengal tiger during a show in Las Vegas. Every year dozens of trainers all over the world are killed or seriously injured by tigers. There is never any sign that the fatal blow or bite is coming, and very often the animal will have performed the same trick a hundred times. It is sufficient for a particular position to irritate the predator (for a predator it remains), and it will attack. In March 2001, also in Las Vegas, a Safari Wildlife tiger killed its trainer, who was grooming it for a commercial, even though this particular animal had been doing photo sessions in public for many years.

THE ROLLING OF THE TIGER'S EYE, WHILE
   HE WAS DEVOURING THE MASSIVE LUMP OF MEAT AND BONE,
      CLUTCHED BETWEEN HIS FOREPAWS, SEEMED TO POSSESS
         THE BRILLIANCY AS WELL AS THE RAPIDITY OF LIGHTNING.

ALFRED BUNN, 19TH-CENTURY THEATRICAL MANAGER

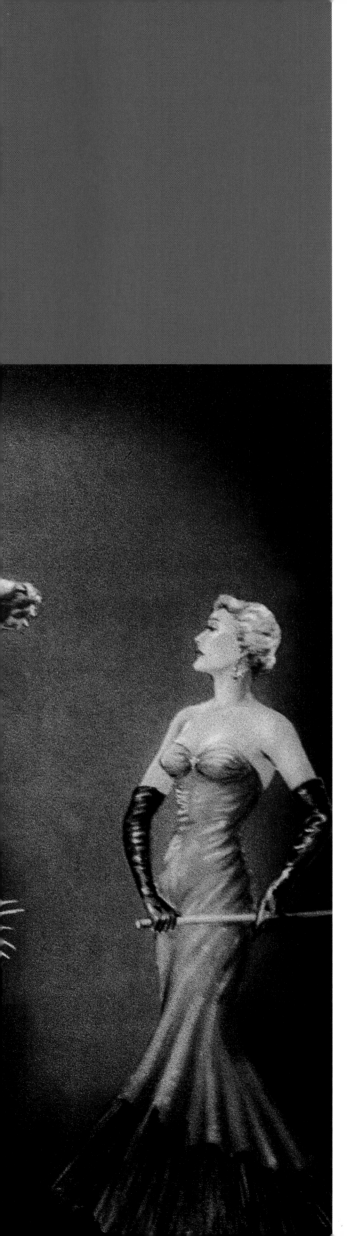

covered their heads and part of their trunks.... Initially the tiger that was to fight them was held back by two leashes, in such a way that it was unable to leap forward and the first elephant that approached was able to deliver two or three blows of its trunk to the tiger's back. The shock was so severe that the tiger was knocked over and stayed motionless on the ground for some time, as if it were dead. However, as soon as it was untied, even though this first attack had quietened its rage, it let out a terrible roar and tried to launch itself at the trunk of the elephant that was advancing to strike it – but the elephant skilfully pulled back its trunk and concealed it behind its tusks.'

In Naples, around 1775, tigers, bulls, lions and bears fought one another. In Spain they still remember the tale of the enraged bull that fought a tiger in honour of the Prince of Austria, who was visiting the court of Philip IV.

The Pomp of Princes

The Chinese used to stage fights between crickets, and even wrote learned treatises and manuals on the subject, but for all that, they could not and did not ignore the tiger that was so popular throughout South-East Asia. In Vietnam there still stands a royal arena built in 1830 during the reign of King Minh Mang. Unique in South-East Asia, this circular enclosure stands on a hill and was used mainly for fights between tigers and elephants. The last of these took place in 1904.

In the 17th century, a Frenchman named François Bernier journeyed to the Indies and found a collection of animals at the court of the Great Mogul Aurangzib. Buffalo were trained to fight tigers, and for this purpose, high earth walls had been erected. The fights would be watched by the ladies of the court, the nobles

Opposite: Founded in England in 1854, Pinder's Circus settled in France a year later. Specializing in equestrian acts, they extended the repertoire by presenting various species of wild animals in acts that were only made possible by erecting tall fences round the circus ring.

Overleaf: From Europe to Asia, as can be seen from this Japanese print, tigers were originally displayed to the public in movable cages, in which the trainer performed his dangerous act.

It is not part of a true culture to tame tigers,
     any more than it is to make sheep ferocious.

HENRY DAVID THOREAU

and the ordinary people. There too, tigers served as proof of the grandeur of princes, and wherever the court went, the menagerie would follow. In Persia, when tigers were not being used for fighting, they were trained to hunt. Transported in cages on the backs of elephants, they were released as soon as the quarry was sighted. The tiger took its own share of the prey, and the rest would be recovered for the hunting party.

It was in southern Italy, during the reign of Frederick II in the 13th century, that the first great European menageries were set up. Some may have been inspired by the accounts of Marco Polo, who spent thirty years travelling across Asia and in 1295 described the tigers and other exotic animals that were found in the palaces of the mighty.

Fighting in the Streets

Echoing the spectacles of ancient times and the courts of the Asian princes, street fights first took place in Europe in the 19th century. It was in England, paradoxically the country in which animal welfare first took root in 1824, that the nobility first began to revel in these sporting entertainments. They were banned in England in the middle of the 19th century, but carried on officially in France until 1863. Butchers' assistants used to organize the shows at several locations in Paris, including the famous Place du Combat – renamed Place du Colonel-Fabien in 1945 – where fights between tigers and mastiff dogs were once held. The animals from the menagerie at the Parc de Vincennes acted out the violent fantasies of the bloodthirsty mob. The park was created in 1654 by Mazarin, and its domestic animals were very quickly replaced by tigers and leopards that were either purchased or given as presents by foreign ambassadors. In 1682,

for instance, a Moroccan VIP made a gift of a 'sweet and gentle' tigress. In honour of the Dauphin, a fight was staged between this beast and a cow, but it was the cow that won! The nobles used to sit in galleries above the animals' quarters, and they would watch the fights taking place down below in the centre of the park.

Zoos and Menageries

Hunting, circuses, arena sports, fights – all of these were closely connected with the concept of the menagerie, which in turn was the result of a powerful human desire to possess, collect and exploit animals. This combination of curiosity and fascination is the basis of mankind's appropriation and domestication of many species. In fact it was in sacred menageries that wild animals were first kept in captivity. The Egyptians set up the earliest zoos 3,400 years ago in Thebes, and gave preferential treatment to their sacred animals – crocodiles, monkeys, oxen, cats – as these were believed to be earthly incarnations of their gods. Similar zoos appeared in many great empires that followed. Assyria, Babylon, ancient Persia, and the Aztecs all collected quantities of animals and

Above: A tiger wrestling a soldier from the French *Infanterie de Marine*. At any moment the big cat might take control.

Opposite: Although at the end of the 19th century, trainers began to devise methods that combined kindness with firmness, the vast majority cowed their animals into submission with blows, deprivation and fear. Here the trainer Charles is performing at a fair.

Man is in no way inferior to the tiger
or the hyena in pitilessness and cruelty.

ARTHUR SCHOPENHAUER

Above: In many parts of Hindustan, as in Greece and Mesopotamia in earlier times, travelling exhibitions of wild animals went to towns and villages, displaying captive tigers to a public that was eager for spectacle.

Opposite: The colonization of Asian countries filled the zoos of Europe with exotic species such as the tiger. Today, every large city has its own zoo.

human freaks, thus demonstrating their desire and ability to master the living world.

The Greeks were the first people to espouse democracy, peace and compassion, and they developed a different concept of human power, so that from the time of their independence they possessed no collections of animals in captivity. Indeed it was from Greece that the Western concept of respect for animals emerged.

The first public zoos appeared in Italy during the 16th century. The sight of exotic animals on display was so inspiring that Louis XIV of France adopted it for the gardens of Versailles, as an entertainment for the aristocracy. Tigers were on show there (having been unknown to the West throughout most of the Middle Ages), along with camels, elephants, zebras and rhinoceros. The allure of menageries grew ever stronger along

with the violence of the animal fights and the grandeur of the private collections, but these zoos eventually took on a more democratic role and became educational tools. Influential cities (London, Berlin, Paris) built their own zoos, which still functioned as showcases of the power of their directors, but at least had the virtue of exhibiting animals rather than sacrificing them in a pool of blood.

Hunters and Exhibitors

In the early 18th century, the menagerie at Schönbrunn in Austria prided itself on the possession of a male Bengal tiger. Some French visitors who saw it told this tale in a report written in 1806: 'Normally he is fed on meat from the butcher's, but when he is suffering from his sickness [a kind of ophthalmia], he is given young, live animals whose warm blood helps to cure him. A few

YOU CAN TAKE THE TIGER OUT OF THE JUNGLE,
BUT YOU CAN'T TAKE THE JUNGLE
OUT OF THE TIGER!

BILL WATTERSON, *CALVIN AND HOBBES*

weeks ago, he was thrown a young dog from the butcher's…. When the dog had recovered from its initial shock, it went up to the tiger and began to lick his eyes; the tiger enjoyed this so much that he forgot his love of killing, and not only spared the dog's life, but also showed his gratitude by nuzzling it…. From this moment on, the two animals have been living in perfect harmony together, and before touching his food, the tiger always waits until his companion has grabbed the choicest morsels.'

The menagerie at the Jardin des Plantes in Paris was built in 1793, as part of the French National Museum of Natural History. This combination was the first step towards a scientific approach, for it was the era when species were first being classified. However, the enterprise still bore witness to the imperialistic desire to conquer nature that had also marked the eagerness of the West to colonize the rest of the world. It was the colonists, in fact, who helped to fill the zoos of Europe by importing large numbers of wild animals from Africa and Asia. But menageries were a major factor in advancing scientific research, allowing the domestication of some species, and increasing our knowledge of the behaviour and the biology of exotic animals.

The Birth of the Circus

While the menageries offered the city-dwellers the edifying spectacle of wild beasts in captivity, animal trainers were touring the provincial towns and villages just as they had done in the Middle Ages. In all respects they were like the men of Hindustan, but instead of bears and wolves, they earned their fame with tigers. The cats were simply tied with a cord to the belt of their master or were hobbled on carts. Their impact on the public, though considerable at first, soon faded when the circus as we know it came on the scene.

It was in England at the end of the 18th century that the modern circus was born, thanks to an English horseman and cavalry sergeant named Philip Astley. These shows needed space for the horses that were to perform in them, and so the arena covered an area some 13 metres (over 40 feet) in diameter. In the 1820s, the invention of the big top enabled man and beast to perform in many different places, and from then on the shows quickly began to grow. New attractions such as lion- and tiger-taming were added to the horse-riding acts. Initially, tigers were exhibited to the public in cages at the entrance to the circus, and the trainer's act was to enter the cage. One of the first of these performers was a famous French trainer named Henri Martin. The next important stage was the invention of a movable cage that could be placed in the centre of the ring. It was not until 1888 that lions and tigers were finally let loose inside a ring cage, erected in sections around the edge of the ring. This novelty entailed a major change

Opposite: Tigers on a circus poster designed by the Polish artist Wiktor Gorka.

Overleaf: In 1923, one of the most famous trainers, Alfred Court, performed an act that included eight lions, four polar bears, a Tibetan bear, three tigers, and two Great Danes. Here the trainer symbolizes the West conquering the wildness of nature.

HOW PITIFUL, HOW IGNORANT
TO SAY THAT ANIMALS ARE MACHINES
DEVOID OF KNOWLEDGE AND FEELING.

VOLTAIRE

in the work of the trainer, as he was now able to deal with large groups of big cats that could perform tricks much as the horses did. They were trained to seem ferocious (engaging in mock fights with the tamer), or affectionate (with the tamer lying next to them or playing with them), or to do acrobatics, such as jumping through hoops of fire. At that time the trainers often dressed as clowns. Many trainers became famous: Isaac Van Amburgh (who performed for Queen Victoria), Alfred Court, Claire Heliot, Thomas Batty, and Ellen Blight, who was killed on 11 January 1850 by a tiger that she had whipped when it failed to perform a trick.

Softly, Softly

In around 1885, Jean-Baptiste Pezon first displayed a non-violent form of animal-training to the Parisian public. Unlike most of his fellow trainers, he did not use a whip, fire or the usual loud noises to frighten his animals. His method was to treat them with kindness and gentleness, and it made him famous as well as inspiring many imitators. However, this did not prevent a campaign being launched in England during the 20th century by the Jack London Club to ban the training of wild animals. It based its case on the work of this famous American writer, who described the odious and brutal methods that had generally been used by trainers to break the will of

their animals. The traditional circus began to lose its appeal in the 1960s, but is now finding new forms to ensure its survival. Public attitudes and sensitivities have changed, and the training of wild animals has been banned in several countries – notably Sweden (in 1988), Norway, Finland, India (since 1998) and Brazil. In Singapore, there has been a ban on the appearance of wild animals in touring shows since 1 January 2002.

Opposite: Within this delightful tiger cub lies the genetic heritage of thousands of generations of life in the wild. Even if it is brought up among humans, it will never lose its predatory nature.

Below: Throughout history, pet tigers have been part of everyday life at court and also in private families. This photo was taken in Java in 1926.

WILD ANIMALS AS PETS

It is a sad paradox that there are now more tigers in captivity than in the wild. There are currently more than 7,000 in private zoos in North America, mainly in Texas. Incidents happen every year because people forget the tiger's savage nature. To be well-balanced, an animal must know the codes of conduct that relate to its own species, and be able distinguish itself from the human world. Letting a tiger sleep in a bed is like having a dog that bosses its masters and ends up biting both them and its fellow dogs. But in the case of a tiger, the outcome is often fatal. According to the Canadian organization Global Action Network, almost 220 people were injured or killed in the last ten years by wild animals kept in captivity by private individuals, or by private and public zoos. In 2001 in Texas, a child of three was snatched by a so-called tame tiger from the arms of an adult.

The Tiger's Lair

The accounts written by the earliest naturalists conveyed an image that bore little resemblance to the real lives of tigers. What do we really know about these predators? How do they live, and why do they still attack human beings, just as their sabre-toothed cousins used to do? The history of the tiger is connected to our own, and if the species does not survive, we will be directly responsible. Will we one day have to learn to live without tigers?

A big noise in the jungle

Tigers are the biggest cats on earth, and also the best adapted to a predatory lifestyle. They are also the only cats to have put human beings on their menu, and have done so ever since our ancestors shared their territory.

The tall grass is waving in the breeze. Over in the clear waters of a stream, two tigers are splashing.

They have just managed to escape from the fire that men have lit in the forest, intending to smoke them out and kill them. Such is the fate of the man-eater. But tigers are cunning, and they have already foiled the plans of their pursuers. Now the roles are reversed. Unseen, the tigers watch the movements and gestures of the men who are trying to track them. Their coats blend in with the vegetation, and the men sense that they are being watched, and soon become uneasy – the tigers' presence is all too palpable. All the other animals fall silent, for when the tiger has you in its sights, it is too late.

Cousins and Ancestors

Some 60 to 35 million years ago, during the Tertiary period, a small tree-dwelling animal about the size of a weasel lived in the forests. It was one of a group of primitive carnivores known as the miacids,

which had the unusual feature of retractable claws. From North America these creatures spread throughout Eurasia via what is now the Bering Strait during the Eocene epoch, some 40 million years ago. Various species evolved from the miacids and in turn gave rise to the current branches of the carnivores. One subgroup must have been the origin of the modern felines. On the tree of evolution, other branches led to the famous sabre-toothed tigers, some of which appeared during the Oligocene epoch, 37 million years ago. These were certainly the most powerful cats that ever roamed the planet. Their razor-sharp teeth grew to an average length of 15 cm (6 inches), and were needed to tear open the massive creatures on which they fed – generally the size of a young mammoth. The best-known of these cats was the Smilodon, which lived in North America about two million years ago. It was approximately the same size as the modern African lion, but its muscles and the different proportions of its body would have made it even stronger. We know that the smilodon could roar, and one study of the fossilized bones shows that, like modern tigers, it hunted both humans and animals either by chasing them or by lying in wait for them. Compressions in the vertebrae at the neck, thorax and hindquarters reveal the enormous strain of leaping from its hiding-place onto its startled prey. There are also indications of chronic traumas and lesions caused by shocks in the area of the chest, the ribs and the spinal column. These traces bear witness to

Above: Man-eaters have roamed the forests for tens of thousands of years, but generally tigers prefer to attack their natural prey, so long as the resources available have not been plundered by the local human population.

Opposite: To kill man-eating tigers, humans have often burned down large sections of the forest. Similar methods were used to kill the wolves of Europe in the Middle Ages.

No man can tame a tiger
into a kitten by stroking it.
Franklin D. Roosevelt

the repeated, violent impact that must have occurred whenever the animal attacked and killed its prey. Inside a cave in Texas, researchers exhumed the fossilized bones and teeth of more than thirty smilodons, as well as several hundred young mammoths.

During that era, perhaps owing to the fact that they had a common ancestor, these cats lived side by side with giant hyenas, with which they shared a surprising number of characteristics – including the number and structure of their teeth. They were already sworn enemies of mankind, their relentless hunter. The last smilodons died out barely 10,000 years ago, at the end of the last ice age. Their disappearance from the planet seems to have been a direct consequence of the extinction of the great ungulates and mammoths of the Pleistocene epoch.

Nevertheless, the evolution of the family *Felidae* – divided into three subfamilies: *Pantherinae* (including the tiger, lion, leopard, jaguar and snow leopard), *Acinonychinae* (the cheetah), and *Felinae* (the domestic cat, puma, ocelot and lynx) – continued unabated.

From the Taiga to the Mangroves

The tiger as a species was born about two million years ago in Asia. It spread and adapted itself to an astonishing variety of climates and habitats, though always preferring

Previous pages: Very sensitive to heat, the tiger often bathes to keep cool. It is an excellent swimmer, able to cross rivers several kilometres wide. It is also capable of swimming up to boats and carrying off the people sitting in them.

Opposite: The shortened shape of the tiger's skull gives extra strength to its jaws.

The Old Tiger and the Hare
– A Tale from Korea

Once upon a time there was an old ti
in the hills of the province of G
One day he met a hare, and said
'I'm hungry! I'm going to eat

The cunning hare thought of
'Do you see those fish in the rive
to the tiger. 'You only have to dip yo
water and close your eyes. If you k
open, it will frighten the fish. S
and don't move your tail until I tell you to. Your
tail will make a magnificent fishing rod.'
The tiger saw the fish in the river, dipped his tail
in the water, and waited patiently. 'You will
soon feel your tail become very heavy,'
added the hare before running away.

Evening came, and the river began to freeze.
When the tiger tried to lift his tail, he smiled
with satisfaction and said: 'I must have caught lots of
fish. It is so heavy that I can't even move it any more.'

Opposite: Different cultures have looked on the tiger with varying degrees of favour. In this 18th-century painting, the painter Sim Sajong
has given it the appearance of a large and rather likeable cat. At that time, the name 'tiger' was often used to refer to any big cat with markings.

WHEN THE TIGER'S AWAY,
THE MONKEYS ARE KINGS OF THE MOUNTAIN.

CHINESE PROVERB

a dense cover of forest. This is why it is found today in the taiga, in tropical forests both wet and dry, and even in mangrove swamps. These different adaptations gave rise to eight subspecies of tiger, three of which are now extinct. Today tigers are found in Bangladesh, Bhutan, Cambodia, China, North Korea (if not already extinct), India, Indonesia (Sumatra), Laos, Malaysia, Myanmar (formerly Burma), Nepal, Russia, Thailand and Vietnam. The colour and thickness of their fur, and also their size, vary according to their geographical origin. Those that live in the hottest regions of India are more colourful than those from China or Siberia. While the Sumatran tiger, which rarely weighs more than 150 kg (330 lbs), is the smallest, its Siberian cousin can claim to be the heavyweight champion of the species, sometimes rising to 380 kg (830 lbs), and measuring 4 m (13 ft) in length. The stripes, which are perfect camouflage in tall grass or thickets, vary in size and number from one individual to another, and no two tigers have the same facial pattern. These designs are the principal method used to tell tigers apart. As a carnivorous predator, the tiger stands at the top of the food chain: it feeds on deer, wild boar and cattle, as well as on smaller prey such as badgers, lynx (in Siberia), birds, and even frogs, tortoises and crabs. It is the sole ruler over its hunting grounds, which may cover an area of 50 sq.km (20 sq. miles) in India, and up to 1,000 sq. km (400 sq. miles) in

the vast forests of Russia. Every tiger has its own territory, which it regularly designates by means of scent markers (urine, faeces, anal secretions, tufts of fur) and visual signals, such as claw marks on trees, which serve both as a boundary and as a visiting card.

Any visiting tiger that sniffs these scents and imbibes their molecular messages – known as pheromones – will receive a lot of information concerning the identity of the resident. He can tell if it is a fertile female, a mature male, or an ageing animal that might have been driven out of its territory. If a tiger fails to mark out its territory every three weeks, that will be sufficient reason for a neighbour to come and take it over. All these clues are analysed by a scent organ called the vomeronasal organ, which is situated on either side of the palate. To use it, the tiger appears almost to grimace, its mouth half-open in an action known as flehmen. The territory of a male will encompass that of several females, and although the male may lose his dominion, each female will

Opposite: Tigers can be found in many different climates, but always where they have the protection of the forest. While the Bengal tiger can withstand very high temperatures, the Siberian tiger can live at temperatures below –50° C.

Overleaf: In the heat of the day, tigers in the jungles of South-East Asia like to be close to running water. They stretch out nearby, and sometimes look out for their prey, allowing them to eat and drink at the same time.

THE TIGER FAMILY

In the family of the Felidae, genus *Panthera*, eight subspecies of tiger have been identified: the Bengal tiger (*Panthera tigris tigris*), the Siberian or Amur tiger (*Panthera tigris altaica*), found in Russia, north China and very rarely North Korea, the Indo-Chinese tiger (*Panthera tigris corbetti*), currently found in Cambodia, Malaysia, Thailand, Vietnam, Laos and Myanmar (formerly Burma), the Sumatran tiger (*Panthera tigris sumatrae*) on the island of that name, and the South China tiger (*Panthera tigris amayensis*). Three subspecies became extinct during the 20th century (see page 129): the Javan tiger (*Panthera tigris sandaicae*), the Bali tiger (*Panthera tigris balica*) and the Caspian tiger (*Panthera tigris virgata*).

THE TIGER RELIES ON THE FOREST,
THE FOREST RELIES ON THE TIGER.
CAMBODIAN PROVERB

normally remain there throughout her reproductive life.

A Fatal Proximity

This mainly solitary way of life forces individual tigers to choose their habitat in areas that are spaced out from one another. The density of the population will be determined by the amount of prey available, and in turn this will depend on the quality and quantity of vegetation. It is essential that nothing should disturb this ecological balance. If there is some kind of deterioration in the habitat, leading to a reduction in the amount of prey, and if there is an increase in the presence of humans and their activities (agriculture, livestock farming, deforestation, hunting), in due course this will lead to a fatal confrontation between the tiger and mankind.

Unfortunately, this is what is happening in all the regions that are inhabited by the tiger, including the vast forests of Russia. Peter Matthiessen, an author who specializes in the Siberian tiger, has reported on a number of cases over the last twenty years in which hunters have fallen victim to tigers. A local witness to one of these attacks reported: 'All found there was a rifle, a cartridge belt, part of the clothing, the hunter's skull, and leg in the high boot.' The origin of the conflict is the same everywhere. It all started at the beginning of the 19th century, when colonization by the West brought a massive increase in human activities to previously wild

Opposite: When hunting, the tiger can cover several dozen kilometres in a night. There are four stages in the hunt: lying in wait, with its striped fur providing perfect camouflage in the grass, the silent approach, the lightning attack, and the kill.

WHEN IT HAS KILLED A MAN WITH A VIOLENT BLOW
FROM ITS PAW, BREAKING THE CLAVICLES, IT BEGINS
AT THE THIGHS, THE STOMACH AND THE CHEST,
THEN IT EATS THE SHOULDERS, THE BACK, THE
LIMBS AND THE HEAD, WHICH IT CRACKS LIKE A NUT.

NIKOLAI BAIKOV, *Big Game Hunting in Manchuria*

regions. In 1906, a French hunter and administrator, Fernand Millet, had been sent on a mission to Annam, and reported that during the construction of a railway, man-eating tigers had chosen to make their home all around the site, which ran along the only river in the region. The water was, of course, necessary for their survival, and as it became increasingly difficult for them to find food, they took to sneaking up on the huts at night and dragging off the workers. 'Sometimes a wild beast would enter a grass hut where natives would be sleeping side by side. It would seize one by the leg, quietly pull him off his mattress, and then choke him before carrying him off. It would never carry off a victim that put up a fight.... The next day, we would go and look for the body. Along the way, we found pieces of leather sticking to the brambles, and then some scraps of clothing, and finally the remains of the corpse, whose thighs had already been eaten.... Stealing cattle and digging up human remains were often the main occupation of the tigers that lived near the villages. These beasts, which live in constant, close proximity to people, end up losing all fear of human beings, and do not hesitate to come in broad daylight and carry off children or women walking or working just a few steps away from their huts.'

A Taste for Human Flesh

During the 1930s in India, villagers did not regard the tiger as their enemy. Its presence in the neighbourhood prevented the herbivores on which it fed from destroying their crops. However, when the British massacred the tigers in a particular region, the villagers were forced to abandon their fields and to go elsewhere, because the pillagers (wild boar, deer, antelope) simply became too numerous to control. Under colonial influence, the peaceful cohabitation between species began to fall apart. 'The ever-growing population has destroyed wildlife more and more rapidly,' wrote Bengt Berg, a hunter in India at the beginning of the 20th century. 'The speed of this process is proportionate to the increase in measures taken by the excellent British administration to counter

Above: A tiger always attacks from the rear or the side.

Opposite: 'Drink deep, Shere Khan, for when wilt thou drink again?' – Rudyard Kipling, *The Jungle Book*

Overleaf: The Bengal tiger is the subspecies with the reddest fur. There were 40,000 of these animals in 1947, but by the end of the 1960s, the number had dwindled to less than 2,000.

famine…. The countryside is cleared, and then with firearms the new inhabitants destroy the animals that damage their crops. The Hindu beliefs that forbid the killing of animals are crumbling. Sooner or later, the tiger finds itself face to face with man, but even when this happens, a tiger will only become a man-eater as a last resort.' People were attacked on the territory of

Above: Travelling by sedan chair – a common scene in Indo-China, *c.* 1907.

Opposite: Forced to kill humans and livestock because of a shortage of its natural prey, the tiger does not hesitate to enter villages in search of food.

the big cat, almost always in broad daylight. It would pounce on them from behind, after creeping up on them slowly and silently, or it would lie in wait. The less dangerous humans became, the more easily the tiger could repeat the process. Observers noted that some man-eaters were handicapped by injuries that prevented them from hunting their natural prey. There were also tigers young and old that were starving because they had been driven out by their fellow cats to the very edges of a territory. In such cases, domestic cattle and human beings were their only chance of survival. During the 20th century,

tigers were said to have caused the deaths of several thousand people in Asia. No other carnivore in the world has been responsible for so many human deaths.

Guardian of the Sunderbans

The mangrove swamps of the Sunderbans – meaning 'beautiful forest' – lie on the border between Bengal and India, in the biggest delta in the world, where the sacred rivers of the Ganges and the Brahmaputra converge. The heart of this vast expanse of islands is criss-crossed by streams and channels, and flooded every day by the tide from the Gulf of Bengal, and here live some 500 tigers. For two hundred years, men and women have lived in dangerous proximity to the wild animals. It is a unique phenomenon. Here more than anywhere else, human beings are the main dish on the tiger's menu. It attacks around 300 victims a year – a habit that appears to have been passed down from one generation to the next. Some specialists believe that it is actually the mother tigers who teach their young by example. But whatever the reason, the fact is that in the Sunderbans the tiger's life is inextricably bound up with that of his human neighbours, and from childhood onwards, the belief system of the local people incorporates the prospect of dying between the paws of the great cat.

The villagers eke out their existence by exploiting the resources of the forest and the waters: timber, fishing, and harvesting wild honey. Honey is the second most important food for young children, after milk, and is also the principal dish that accompanies the dead into the afterlife. Barely a day passes when a fisherman, a woodsman or a honey-gatherer is not injured or killed by a tiger. In the summer months, the giant Himalayan bees – one of the

DANGER IN SUMATRA

Between 1972 and 1975, there were still around a thousand tigers on the island of Sumatra. Within a few years, the ravages of poaching decimated the population, their habitat was destroyed, and their prey killed. At the same time, attacks began on human beings. Today there are barely 400 tigers left in Sumatra, divided between five reserves. Between a current human population of 60 million and the tiger, which needs a lot of living space, a balance is very hard to achieve.

It is not the ape, nor the tiger in man that I fear, but the donkey.

William Temple, American ecologist

most aggressive species in the world – build their hives and fill their combs with the precious nectar. This is the time when the native people collect the honey, and before they set out, they hold a ceremony dedicated to the gods of the forest – Vishnu, Daksin Ray, and the mother goddess that protects the woods. The ceremony is called the *Pudja*. At the prow of the boat, the shaman sets up a kind of altar, and there he repeats the mantras that are believed to protect his people against the tiger. The women standing on the shore watch their menfolk disappear in their boat, and all of them join in the prayers. And when each season comes to an end, and the honey, wood and fish have been brought home, it often happens that yet another village of widows, *vidhaba pallis*, must be added to the list of those for which the government must take responsibility.

Because of the low vegetation and the mud, the men often get stuck, and most of the time they are bent double, in a posture like that of the animals. Hidden in the tall grass, the tiger will attack without warning just as the hunters enter or leave the forest. But if the men change their tactics, the tiger adapts to them, just as it does when hunting any other prey. In recent years, the government has tried all kinds of devices. Electrified puppets that looked like villagers were set up at strategic points. The intention was to give the tiger a nasty shock, so that it would learn its lesson and stop attacking anything shaped like a human. This worked for a while, but soon became ineffective. Face masks worn on the nape of the neck did not impress the tiger either, though it never attacks a human being from the front. And if it does not hunt people on the ground, it will hunt them in the water, for it is an excellent swimmer, and can cover up to 15 kilometres (9 miles) at sea, and double that in a river. Some have even been known to climb into boats and carry men off while they were sleeping. In 1670, a Frenchman named François Bernier reported on just such an instance of this vicious mode of attack.

What has driven the tigers to behave in this way? Different people have put forward different theories. Hubert Hendrichs, a German researcher, attributed the tigers' exceptional irascibility to a lack of fresh water. Excess salt, he argued, would cause organic disorders. Others suggest a hyper-territoriality, or even a highly developed taste for human flesh, encouraged by the fact that in this region dead bodies may be left to float with the current, as is the tradition in many parts of India.

Opposite: If you should happen to come face to face with a tiger, the last thing you should do is turn your back and run away. Such an action will actually rouse its hunting instincts. If you stand perfectly still, the animal may well continue on its way.

Three extinct subspecies

The Caspian tiger's territory once extended from eastern Turkey to the frontiers of Iran and Afghanistan and as far as Mongolia. The species died out in the 1960s, because of intensive poaching, deforestation, and the disappearance of its prey. The Bali tiger suffered the same fate, becoming extinct in the 1940s. Large-scale hunting to supply the zoo trade was the cause of its disappearance, and by the time the government passed legislation to protect the breed, it was already too late. Regarded as dangerous, the Javan tiger was hunted throughout the 19th century. Reserves were set up when its habitat was destroyed, but it died out some thirty years ago.

The art of being a tiger

Nature has not made the tiger a simple creature governed by its instincts, like the majority of animals. This big cat has evolved in a world where every individual demonstrates awareness, emotion, skill and intelligence all its own.

Opposite: Two brothers rub their heads against each other's necks to express affection.

Dawn breaks over the ruined temple, and the first rays of sun light up the sky.

At the top of a banyan tree, a macaque is looking anxiously around, and utters a piercing bark. In a moment, the panic spreads to all the animals at all levels of the forest. The birds screech, the monkeys hurtle through the trees, and down at ground level the noise and bustle are just as chaotic as up above. And then the tigress appears, majestically descending the vine-covered steps of the temple, with a heavy, self-assured tread and a low growl, exuding strength, grace and beauty.

A Wild Wedding

The tiger reaches sexual maturity at the age of three or four. A female on heat patrols her territory, roaring loudly to summon the male. When the two of them meet, she seduces her partner with a series of flirtatious games, nuzzles, provocative poses – all designed to tease her suitor. But as soon as he dares to make his move, he will generally find himself getting the brush-off. Undeterred, he will accept the humiliation. Despite the intense excitement, he is the model of patience. And when at last the great moment of union arrives, the male mounts the female, and grips her nape between his teeth so that she cannot move or bite. The sexual act lasts between 15 and 20 seconds, and is repeated up to one hundred times over the next two or three days, when the tigress is receptive. After this, she distances herself from the male to keep herself safe during her pregnancy.

After 103 days, she gives birth to a litter of between two and seven cubs, each weighing about a kilo, and she suckles them for two months. Many cubs die at an early age, which is why mothers with more than two cubs are rarely seen. During the first few weeks, she frequently changes her location – up to five times a month – in order to escape the attentions of predators. At the age of four weeks, the cubs start to eat meat, which she predigests and regurgitates for them. Two weeks later, their birth weight will have quintupled, and from that moment on they can attack the small, live creatures that she brings to them. A mother and her cubs are generally the basic family unit among tigers.

Above: At the beginning of the 20th century, there were more than 100,000 tigers living in the wild. Since then the number is estimated to have dropped to 5,000. Each new litter is a small miracle.

Opposite: The female gently carries her young in her mouth. During the first few weeks, she frequently changes the location of her lair in order to prevent other predators from spotting them. It is rare to see a tigress with more than two cubs, so high is the mortality rate.

ITS FACE WAS RED WITH BLACK
AND WHITE MARKS, AND ITS BELLY
WHITE; WITH ITS TAIL LIKE
A LIONESS, IT LOOKED A
PRODIGY OF FEROCITY.

JOSAPHAT BARBARO, 15TH-CENTURY VENETIAN MERCHANT

Opposite: All tigers are excellent climbers, but each one has a different temperament. In a litter you will generally find one bold and dominant cub, and one that is timid and submissive.

Previous pages. At the age of six weeks, it is time for a cub to explore its mother's territory, under her supervision.

Family Life

Infanticide by the father is not a characteristic of the tiger. It does exist among other species, notably lions and primates. If a male lion loses his territory, he is driven out and his successor may well kill his cubs or those of the other females present, so that he can impregnate them himself and thus ensure his line of descent. This does not necessarily make him tolerant towards his own cubs, however, and for this reason the lioness will keep her distance and attend solely to the needs of her young.

Observers have noted, however, that male tigers regularly visit their females and their cubs in a relaxed fashion. They play with the cubs, protect them against potential predators, share prey that they have killed, or come and feast on what the tigress has caught. Some tiger specialists, such as the Indian Valmik Thapar, have reported several cases in which the male and the female have hunted together, and similar accounts were written by hunters in South-East Asia during the colonial era. But it does occasionally happen, for various reasons – a difficult pregnancy, lack of food preventing her from suckling the cubs, or some genetic abnormality – that the female eats her own young. A legend among the Moi people of Vietnam tells how the tigress only kills those cubs that she suspects will one day destroy humans and their livestock.

PERHAPS GOD MADE CATS SO THAT MAN MIGHT
HAVE THE PLEASURE OF FONDLING THE TIGER.

ROBERTSON DAVIES, *THE DIARY OF SAMUEL MARCHBANKS*

Learning Through Play

Games are the most important method by which a tiger learns to be a tiger. They promote speed and intelligence and performance skills, and they show the limits that cannot be exceeded and the social structures that must be adhered to. Mock fights, for instance, teach the cubs how to control their aggressive instincts. They rehearse all the rituals that will be necessary when they have grown up to prevent them from killing one another. Games are a universal language, and they are a vital step on the path to independence. A piece of fruit, a pebble, a small animal – all of these will help to train coordination, to strengthen the muscles and the reflexes, to build up stamina – in short, to teach the cub to become one of the mightiest of all predators. A cub will use up a lot of energy playing these games, and sometimes there are dangers involved – it can become so absorbed in what it's doing that there may be a fatal accident, or it may expose itself to attack by another predator.

The way an animal plays will depend on the species. Those creatures that live in social groups will play different games from those that are destined to live alone, like tigers. While a young antelope may enjoy itself kicking or running around with its fellow antelopes,

young cats prefer to play with objects or small animals. This is evident when you watch kittens at play. The games are a way of rehearsing the moves that will later be useful when the cat lies in wait for its prey, or has to pounce on it.

Tiger cubs remain dependent on their mother until they are 18 months old, and they continue to stay in her territory for a while longer. Not until they are between two and three years old do they leave to make their own way in the world. By then, they have learned all the basic lessons through imitation, and

Above: Like a kitten playing with a ball of wool, the cub is curious about everything that comes within its reach.

Opposite: Feeding, sleeping and playing are the main occupations of the tiger cub.

JEALOUS AS A TIGER

Aristotle, the ancient Greek philosopher, was the first to make the distinction between the five senses, almost 2,500 years ago. Centuries later, Western Christianity condemned the misguided devotion to sensuality and used animals as symbols of sin in works on religious morality. The tiger was traditionally associated with envy or jealousy, while the lion symbolized anger and slander and the bear was considered the embodiment of lust.

THE TIGER PICKED THE DEAD PIG UP IN
ITS FRONT PAWS.... HE WAS PATTING IT
IN A COAXING MANNER, AS A CAT WILL
PAT AT A WIND-BLOWN FEATHER.

ARTHUR LOCKE, *THE TIGERS OF TRENGGANU*

Above: A tiger is capable of attacking a young elephant or rhinoceros. When it captures a buffalo, it aims for the throat and kills within ten minutes. It generally breaks the neck of smaller prey.

Opposite: The tiger is not just a killing machine. It can feel and express anger, joy, fear, compassion and tenderness.

so they are now ready to become hunters themselves.

Hunting Techniques

It is a fact of life that a tiger must kill to eat, and this procedure takes up much of the night, for the quest begins at dusk and ends at dawn. Tigers are indefatigable walkers, and they may cover more than 40 km (25 miles) in their search for food. Every fibre of their being is designed to hunt. The shortened shape of the skull makes the jaws strong; the temporal muscles enable the jaws to lock onto a prey that is struggling, while the eyes face forwards – a feature of great benefit to predators, as it gives them a wide visual field while at the same time allowing them to pinpoint a single detail within a split second. The tiger hunts by lying in wait or by creeping up on its victim, and like most predators it is sensitive to the slightest movement. In the course of

its evolution, its senses and nervous system have become so refined that it can immediately analyse and evaluate the distance and position of its prey. Its brain is thus attuned to everything around it, and as it tracks its prey, it can anticipate every movement. Whether the terrain is dense forest, stony ground or water, and whether the prey is alone or standing on the edge of a herd, the tiger will be able to adapt accordingly. All these talents will combine in the final assault, but the end result will also depend on acquired knowledge and experience.

'A large stag was running through the jungle, leaving behind a trail of broken branches,' reported an experienced hunter in South-East Asia in the 1950s. 'It was running erratically, first in this direction, then in that, as if it was trapped in an enclosure. The tiger, hidden in the vegetation, moved extremely rapidly, cutting off the route of its prey every time the stag tried to follow a line of escape.' The method is always the same. Initially, the silent approach, followed by patient observation that may last for several hours, from positions where it is hidden from view and from any wind that might carry its scent to the prey. As it comes closer, the tension mounts. Its body stiffens, its ears are pinned back against its skull, and its eyes stare. It advances very slowly,

EACH HAS HIS OWN COURAGE, AS HIS OWN
TALENT; BUT THE COURAGE OF THE TIGER
IS ONE, AND OF THE HORSE ANOTHER.

RALPH WALDO EMERSON

lengthening or shortening its stride as necessary, or even freezing. Each of its movements, supported by an extraordinarily flexible spine, evinces that fascinating feline suppleness. And then the moment arrives, and it moves into attack mode, launching itself at lightning speed, almost as if it were flying. The final leap may cover as much as 10 metres (over 30 feet). But it must adjust and control its balance, and coordinate all its movements. It kills its prey by choking it or by severing the spinal cord at the nape of the neck – which demands a very firm grip on the victim. This is done by means of the retractable claws, which can be as long as 10 cm (4 inches) – formidable tools, whose retractability preserves them from wear and tear. This latter feature is operated by elastic ligaments, and as well as enabling the tiger to grip its victim, it can help the animal to climb trees – a legacy from its old tree-dwelling ancestors.

As soon as the prey is dead, the tiger will carry it off to a sheltered spot, where it will normally devour the body, starting with the hindquarters. At a single sitting, it can eat between 8 and 30 kg (17 and 66 lbs) of meat. A tigress with cubs will have to kill an animal every five days, whereas in general a solitary tiger will need one every week or so – 40 to 50 a year. The strength that it uses to move its victim is astonishing. A hunter in Indo-China described how a tigress had dragged the remains of a buffalo into a hiding-place. 'We enlisted the help of eight Malay fishermen, who were used to pulling on ropes, but they were unable to move the beast a single inch, and in the end we had to fetch a wagon with a winch.'

What Do Tigers Dream Of?

When they're not hunting, cats rest or sleep. There's nothing surprising in this, since sleep is common to all the higher animals. One of the privileges of being a powerful predator like the tiger, at the very top of the food chain, is that it can sleep in perfect safety – unlike, say, the hare, which can only afford a break of about 30 seconds. The herbivores on which the predator feeds are biologically programmed to remain on the alert, and so they get far less sleep unless they have found safe shelter. In contrast to fish, amphibians and reptiles, whose temperature depends on the environment, tigers have a stable temperature, and their sleep is characterized by different phases that alternate between slow and rapid wave. During the latter, there are repeated periods of heightened electrical activity in the brain, known as REM (rapid eye movement), and these mark the phases of deepest sleep. The muscles relax, the eyeballs spin, the brain becomes hyperactive – and the sleeper dreams. With lions,

Opposite: The tiger's musculature and its flexible spine function like the string of a bow. It is capable of leaping a distance of 10 to 12 metres (some 30 to 40 feet).

PORTRAYING THE TIGER

The imaginations of European artists were fired from the moment the first tigers were described. First there were the accounts of travellers in the 13th and 14th centuries, and then tigers were imported from Asia in the 16th century. In the 19th century, when Eugène Delacroix painted a horse attacked by a tiger, the big cat still symbolized instincts and passions, whereas the oppressed, domesticated horse it was eating stood for civilization. It was with this imagery in mind that William Blake wrote: 'The tigers of wrath are wiser that the horses of instruction' (from *Proverbs of Hell*).

THE TIGRESS IS A PATIENT TEACHER AND A GOOD
MOTHER. SHE WILL DEFEND HER YOUNG
WITH GREAT COURAGE AND DETERMINATION,
OFTEN ATTACKING THOSE WHO APPROACH THEM
BEFORE THERE IS ANY REAL NEED FOR HER TO DO SO.

ARTHUR LOCKE, *THE TIGERS OF TRENGGANU*

domestic cats and probably tigers too, it is estimated that dreams occupy about 20 per cent of sleeping time, or 200 minutes a day. By comparison, humans dream for only about 100 minutes, chimpanzees for 90 minutes, and chickens and cows for a mere 25 minutes.

What do tigers dream about? It's difficult to say. All that science is certain of is that every animal dreams about elements of its own existence. We may therefore assume that a tiger would dream about its everyday life as a hunter. Cubs dream more than adults, because their nervous system is immature. Dreams will help them to develop, and to remember the experiences and the lessons of each day.

A Memory like a Tiger

'There was consciousness in the living world long before the arrival of man,' writes the behavioural scientist Boris Cyrulnik. 'It is not spiritual, nor is it supernatural, and it is not the result of a combination of neurochemicals. For it to manifest itself, the living creature must respond to representations and not to perceptions. Representations are possible as soon as the phenomenon of memory appears. At that moment, living beings become capable of learning. The capacity of an animal to form an image of itself, to feel emotions, to memorize and to dream

is therefore real, although it is gradated because it varies according to the species.'

This is the reason why two tigers brought up together over a relatively long period of time will be easily able to recognize each other after separation. In the same way, a mother can identify her offspring long after the young ones have gone off on their own. 'The more capable a brain is of representation, the more it can visualize an absent world – that is to say, it can process information from the past, and not merely react to perceptions.'

The Tiger Machine

The Greek philosopher Aristotle wrote a ten-volume study of animals, in which he listed some five hundred species, thus inaugurating the era of scientific observation. He wrote: 'Every realm of Nature is marvellous...so we should venture on the study of every kind of animal without distaste; for each and all will reveal to us something natural and something beautiful. Absence of the haphazard and conduciveness of everything to an end are to be found in Nature's works in the highest degree, and the resultant end of her generations and combinations is a form of the beautiful.' It has, however, taken humanity quite some time to be able to see the tiger from a perspective other than a

Opposite: Studies of feline behaviour and mental processes have established that a tigress and her cubs can recognize one another even long after they have been separated.

Overleaf: It takes a tiger about three years to reach maturity.

Above: Engraving of a tiger from 1869. During the 18th and 19th centuries, tigers were counted and described, but no real attempts were made to study their behaviour.

Opposite: This male tiger perceives the world around him through his highly developed sensory system. Although his senses work in the same way as our own, they are superior in many ways.

subjective one. Long ago, a Chinese author described the tiger as follows: 'It is seven feet long and has a seven-month period of gestation. When it is 500 years old, its fur becomes completely white, and it is said that the tiger may sometimes reach the great age of 1,000 years.' Elsewhere, Islamic beliefs recorded in a 16th-century Arab text describe the tiger in the following terms: 'When it becomes angry, this animal enters into such a rage that all prudence leaves it, and it is capable of exhausting itself and thereby dying. It is proud and stubborn. It has murder in its blood.... It is crazy about rice wine. If man provides it with a sufficient quantity, it gets drunk and falls into a heavy sleep. When a tiger gives birth, each of its young has a serpent wrapped round its neck.... The tiger is capable of leaps varying from one to forty

metres high....' In his *Histoire naturelle*, Buffon (1707–88) gives a rather subjective account: 'Among the class of carnivores, the lion is in first place, the tiger in second. The tiger is despicably ferocious and unjustly cruel. Its body is too long, its legs too short, its head too small, its eyes wild, its tongue the colour of blood, always hanging out of its mouth; the tiger has no traits but those of base wickedness and insatiable cruelty... Even when glutted with meat, it seems always to be thirsting for blood; its rage never rests, other than for the time it spends lying in wait.'

Thanks to modern studies, the absurd idea that animals are governed only by their instincts has long since lost credibility. This concept arose from the 17th- and 18th-century belief that animals were nothing but machines. Each individual grasps the world around it through its own sensory system, which leads it to give specific meanings to the things it perceives. For a tiger, a rotting corpse teeming with worms would therefore seem appetizing, and a human or animal form in a particular position would provoke it to attack. The German naturalist Jacob von Uexküll in the 1930s called this concept of the animal's own world the *Umwelt*. Subsequently, behavioural science has found many such analogies between humans and animals. Strangely, it was the big-game hunters of the early 20th century in the colonies that were the first real tiger ethnologists. To track their prey, these men had to understand its habits. In their accounts the tiger is no longer the embodiment of some far-fetched idea, but an animal with habits, traditions, memory, intelligence and cunning. These records were also the first to give significant details of the ways in which tigers communicate.

Why does the tiger have stripes?

On the edge of a tropical forest, in the centre of Vietnam, lived a group of tigers. They were called 'Lords of the Jungle' or, more intimately, Öng Oop.

One day, the chief tiger watched a buffalo ploughing the land where men grew rice. He asked the buffalo about its master, and was told: 'He is very small, and not very strong, but he has a wisdom that we do not possess.' 'What is a wisdom?' asked the tiger. 'Go and ask him,' replied the buffalo.

The tiger approached the man, trembling. 'I've been told that you have a wisdom, and I would like to see it.' 'Ah!' exclaimed the peasant, 'my wisdom is very valuable, and so I've left it in a box at home because I was afraid of losing it, but if you allow me to, I'll go and fetch it. However, I'm worried about my buffalo — I'm afraid you'll eat it. To set my mind at rest, will you allow me to tie you to this tree?' The tiger agreed. 'Now you see my wisdom!' cried the man, who then launched himself at the tiger with a whip, leaving deep stripes on the tiger's skin. The man was afraid that the tiger would take revenge, and so ever since that day men have instinctively been afraid of the big cat, while tigers cannot look at a man without groaning.

From a Vietnamese folktale by Vinh Luu

Opposite: This tiger was drawn in 1928 by Raoul de la Nézière for a children's book.
It takes a few anatomical liberties, in favour of an imaginative recreation.

Animals live in a world of emotions and sensory representations, and are capable of affection and suffering, but for all that they are not human. Paradoxically, they may teach us the origins of our own behaviour, and the animal nature that remains within us.

Boris Cyrulnik,

The Language of Tigers

Animals have evolved some very varied means of communication – chemical, visual, vocal, tactile, behavioural – which are not limited to our human, verbal language. Tigers use facial expressions that involve the position of the ears and the dilation of the pupils, as well as scents and sounds. Tiger language also uses vocalizations, rhythms and cries, the loudest of which can carry two or three kilometres through the forest. The tiger is talkative, and has a rich register. 'Tigers are able to produce a wide variety of noises, ranging from a spitting, high-powered hiss to a full-throated roar,' wrote Arthur Locke, a lieutenant colonel in Malaysia. 'They grunt; they have a coughing roar and various types of snarls. Sometimes they tend to produce a sound very much like a long, low moan. Occasionally they give vent to their feelings by a sort of complaining, mumbling noise. The calling roar, sounded when a tiger is seeking a mate, or when a tigress is searching for a lost cub, is impossible to describe, possessing as it does such volume, so much that is challenging yet mournful, sinister and majestic. It starts with a long, full-throated sound, ascending the scale slightly. There is a short but clear pause, then a lower, explosive boom. The nearest that I can get to it on paper is "Oooomph – aough".'

The hyoid bone that supports the larynx at the base of the tongue is present in all mammals, and is derived from the bones that once supported the gills of aquatic vertebrates. It functions as a sound amplifier, and it is flexible and cartilaginous in the genus *Panthera*, enabling these big cats, including the tiger and lion, to roar loudly.

The tiger is also able to imitate other animals. 'I heard long ago that the tiger can imitate the cry of the

stag, but I didn't believe it until I actually heard it for myself,' wrote the hunter Plas. 'Another cry is the one it utters when it comes to the bait – a sort of mewing, or prolonged yawn, which is almost nonchalant. I once saw a tiger standing on its hind legs and shaking the branches of a tree with its front paws to drive off the birds of prey that were eating the bait. As it did this, it was uttering sounds that were exactly like those of a wild boar, and that's what I would have taken it for if I hadn't seen the animal with my own eyes.'

Above: Ears pinned back against the skull and pupils dilated is an expression of either fear or menace – the posture is designed to scare off potential opponents.

Opposite: Ed Walsh, a researcher in Omaha, discovered that tigers can emit low-frequency sounds, just as whales and elephants can. This enables them to communicate with each other over long distances.

TIGER TALK

Some forty to fifty types of tiger vocalization have been identified. These include babbling, barking, bawling, bellowing, blaring, bleating, braying, breathing, buzzing, calling, chattering, chuffing (also known as *prusten* – a snort that is unique to the tiger), clamouring, cooing, groaning, growling, grumbling, hissing, howling, humming, mewing, moaning, mumbling, murmuring, muttering, purring, roaring, screaming, screeching, shouting, sighing, sniffing, snivelling, snorting, squeaking, swishing, wailing, weeping, whimpering, whining, whispering, whistling, whooping and yapping.

A beast at bay

Once an emblem of power, the tiger
has now become a symbol of
the wildlife that is disappearing
under the pressure of human
demographics. There is no longer any
room for wild animals. Quite
apart from the tragic destiny of this
great predator, its disappearance
is an alarm signal to remind us of the
interdependence of species. If there
is no future for the tiger, what will
the future be for humanity?

Opposite: Despite international
legislation, official protection
(since 1972) and the establishment
of special reserves, tiger poaching
still continues in many regions.

Near the temple, the great tiger is distracted from its meal by the echo of suspicious sounds.

It gives a muffled growl, and sniffs the air. Now alert, the tigress brings her cubs from out in the open back to the safety of the lair. Close by, two men – armed and noisy – are setting up camp. They are there to profit from the temples and the tigers. They hang their hammocks between

Above: The big cat hides in vain, because there is no escape from the poachers. Every day, hundreds of thousands of people take traditional Chinese medicines derived from the tiger.

Opposite: Even today, the tiger brings a fat profit to the sellers of claws, amulets and medicines. Folk beliefs are helping to bring about the extinction of the species.

the trees. A dog scents the tiger and is terrified – its hair stands on end. The elephant flaps its ears against its skull and trumpets. In fear, the yoked buffalo break their tethers and run away. A tiger is on the prowl. Now it settles to lie in wait, studying the movements of the men. When they reach the galleries of the temple, a terrible roar makes the ruins shake. In the morning, the expedition makes its way back through the jungle, the men heavily laden with the treasures that they have plundered from the temple. The body of the tiger goes with them.

Bones, Meat and Medicines

The Indo-Chinese tiger is dying out. In the forests that cover Cambodia, Malaysia, Myanmar (formerly Burma), Thailand, Vietnam and Laos there are now less than a thousand tigers left. None of the very few

environmental laws issued internationally and intended to protect these big cats and their habitats (1972 in Thailand, 1989 in Laos) have been seriously enforced, mainly because of corruption. In Cambodia – a region economically destabilized by decades of conflict – poaching, big-game hunting and tree-felling are the basis of businesses that are far more profitable in the short term than the conservation of ecosystems. For what profit could a peasant society expect from preserving an animal which, when dead, would provide bones, fur, genitals, whiskers and more, all of which are seen as valuable medicinal commodities in the rich countries of Asia? According to experts, the value of a tiger on the black market is between $60,000 and $200,000, while the monthly wage of a forest warden may be no more than $10. As some seventy tigers a year are killed in order to satisfy the market in China, there are now only a few dozen remaining in Cambodia.

Between the countries that are caught in the poverty trap and the rich ones that are ready to pay enormous prices for their tigers, the fate of the species sadly appears to be sealed. The 100,000 tigers that roamed the world at the beginning of the 20th century have now dwindled to no more than 5,000. The rarer they become, the greater the demand, and the higher the price. Peter Matthiessen writes: 'Between 1975 and 1992 South Korea alone imported 3,720 kg [8,200 lbs] of dried tiger bone from Indonesia...; between 1991 and 1993 South Korea imported 475 kg [1,050 lbs] of bone, or about 20 tigers annually.' According to its size, one tiger will provide between 6 and 12 kg (13 to 26 lbs) of powdered bone. The increasing rarity of the tiger in the wild has led to other illegal practices designed to procure the desired commodities.

A paper tiger frightens nobody.

Chinese proverb

An investigation by the Hong Kong news magazine *Asiaweek* revealed that in the late 1990s live tigers were delivered to restaurants in Taiwan. Some wildlife conservation groups (notably in Thailand) think that the answer lies in tiger farms which, under the pretence of being zoos seeking to conserve the species by breeding it in captivity, in fact exist to satisfy the demand for tiger meat and blood in restaurants and stores, and for other traditional medicinal products. According to the Environmental Agency in Tokyo, two-thirds of the country's pharmacies sell remedies based on tiger body parts. In Amsterdam and New York, 80 per cent of Chinese pharmacies sell the same substances imported from China, although the sale of such products has been officially banned in China since 1993. North Korea and Japan, meanwhile, have simply refused to impose a ban.

Damaging Beliefs

This tragic trade is based around the belief that different parts of the tiger's body possess magical powers. It was once thought that if a warrior wore a tiger's claw, he would be brave and invincible; the whiskers would endow him with strength and courage, and would even make him bulletproof. Between 1930 and 1950 the Chinese became convinced that the tiger's bones contained a substance that was guaranteed to ward off evil spirits and madness. The small bones of the feet attached to a child's wrist would protect it against fits, and if a fever was to be lowered or an evil spirit driven away,

Previous pages: Even Siberia is no longer a haven for wildlife. The reserves have been exploited for timber, which has reduced the territory available to the tigers. They are now dying of starvation owing to the lack of prey.

Opposite: In 1935, the death of an Indo-Chinese tiger was deemed to be of no importance as there were so many of them in the forests. Today less than a thousand survive in the jungles of South-East Asia.

THE SYMPATHY THAT MAN FEELS TOWARDS ALL LIVING
CREATURES IS WHAT TRULY MAKES HIM A MAN.

ALBERT SCHWEITZER

Above: From the pharmacies of the rich Asian countries to the village market stalls, the tiger is the centre of a huge trade based on its supposed medicinal qualities. China is the biggest consumer, along with South Korea.

Opposite: Wine derived from the blood and bones of the tiger is very much in demand. Making poaching illegal will have little effect so long as these legends persist.

there was no better remedy than sitting on a tiger skin – although patients had to be careful not to damage it, or else they might be transformed into a tiger themselves. Even today, it is widely believed that the tiger's penis is an aphrodisiac, that its gallstones mixed with honey will cure abscesses, and its eyes will prevent fits. Rubbing in an oil containing tiger brains can cure acne and even laziness! The tail ground into powder and mixed with soap is good for skin conditions. The bones mixed with wine act as a tonic, as do the ears prepared in a special brew. The collar bones will make a man

stronger than his enemies, while the ribs will simply bring happiness. Eating tiger meat and drinking its blood will immunize against snake bites and will also pass on the animal's strength. The consumption of tigers by the Chinese takes many different forms, and it is embedded in a symbolic and cultural belief system that confers both meaning and power on food or on other substances that are consumed.

From the remote provinces to the business districts of Beijing, the same psychological significance is attached to products derived from the tiger. 'The food consumed is believed to transfer analogically some of its special characteristics to those who eat it,' writes sociologist Claude Fischler. 'This is the principal trait of the belief in magic – the idea that the image equals the object.' In other words, while many Westerners still believe that eating red meat will bring energy and warmth because of the association with the redness of blood, many in China are convinced that by consuming a part of the tiger, in no matter what form, they can also acquire its attributes.

Shrinking Habitats

Shortly before the Second World War, there were still around 4,000 South China tigers. The destruction of their habitat – forests felled, the disappearance of prey, the building of new towns and villages – forced the tiger to encroach increasingly on the human world. In 1959, Mao

SURVIVING TIGER POPULATIONS WORLDWIDE

Bengal tigers: between 2,500 and 3,800 in India, according to various sources; 300–460 in Bangladesh; 150–250 in Nepal; 20–50 in Bhutan. Siberian tigers: perhaps 400 in Russia, northern China and possibly North Korea. South China tigers: 25–80. Sumatran tigers: 400–650. Indo-Chinese tiger: 100–200 in Cambodia, 600–650 in Malaysia, 150–600 in Thailand, 200–300 in Vietnam, and an unknown number in Laos and Myanmar (Burma).

reacted to this by waging a massive campaign of extermination against the animal, seeing it as an enemy of the people. As occurred during the extermination of the wolf in Europe during the 18th century, there were rewards for those who successfully slaughtered tigers. In just one year, 3,000 were killed. Today there are barely thirty left. Experts agree that the South China tiger will be the next subspecies to die out, after the extinction of the Bali tiger in the 1940s, the Caspian tiger in the 1960s, and the Javan tiger in the 1970s (see page 126). It is estimated that there are about 700 tigers in northern Laos, which is a tribute to the animal's amazing adaptability in a country that has been ravaged by war, and large areas of which are still riddled with anti-personnel mines. These weapons are also used by poachers, who place them inside the bodies of animals that tigers like to feed on. When the tiger seizes hold of the bait, the mine explodes.

There are few forest wardens to supervise these large areas of land, and in any case they frequently have no official right to arrest people. They themselves are threatened and often badly paid, and so may well be open to corruption. As well as this almost unchecked poaching, the tiger's last refuges are now being destroyed. Even in nature reserves, the land is often cleared for timber or for farming, automatically reducing the tiger's prey. As for policies that allow the construction of roads through the heart of the forest, and dams that engulf hundreds of thousands of hectares, it appears that the quest for profit blots out all consideration of ecological factors and sustainable development.

'Cambodia has signed up to a law that bans deforestation, and this allows it – as with a number of other countries that have taken such ecological measures – to receive aid

Opposite: An engraving of Western hunters mounted on elephants, 1919. Big-game hunting, started by the British in the 19th century, paved the way to wholesale massacre of tigers and was a major factor in pushing the species to what is now the brink of extinction.

FUTURE GENERATIONS WOULD BE TRULY SADDENED
that this century had so little foresight,
so little compassion, such lack of generosity
of spirit for the future that it would
eliminate one of the most dramatic and
beautiful animals the world has ever seen.

GEORGE SCHALLER, zoologist

THE ANIMAL KINGDOM IS AT A DRAMATIC
TURNING POINT. THOSE THAT COMPETE WITH
US — THE WILD ANIMALS AND THOSE THAT LIVE
INDEPENDENTLY — WILL DISAPPEAR. THE ONLY
ANIMALS LEFT WILL BE THOSE WE KEEP AS PETS,
THOSE WE COSSET, THOSE WE EAT, AND THOSE
WE ABANDON AT ROADSIDE SERVICE STATIONS.

JEAN-JACQUES ANNAUD

from the United Nations,' writes Jean-Jacques Annaud. 'But at the same time, the country has accepted from China an offer to cancel its debts on condition that it allows the construction of a six-lane highway across Mondolkiri, the last forested massif in the region. In a few years, there will not be a single tree left standing. And if there are no more trees, and no more vegetation, there will be no more prey and there will be no more tigers.'

The great predators have always had to pay the price for the so-called progress of civilization. They have become undesirable whenever mankind has commandeered land for economic purposes. In South-East Asia, China and India, the values upheld by the animist peoples are dismissed by younger generations. At best, the tiger represents a useful means of improving their financial circumstances. But of course, it is all too easy to condemn this attitude when one is not living in direct contact with tigers. It is also crucial to take into account the distress and confusion of people – for the most part forced to live in appalling conditions – when they are faced with international bodies that pump vast amounts of money into the conservation of an animal that kills both themselves and their livestock. All those organizations that seek to protect the tiger and its environment

agree that conservation programmes cannot succeed without first taking into account the economic, social and political problems of the local population, and without convincing them of the good sense and the potential benefits of such an operation. India is a prime example.

Mrs Gandhi's Reserves

As a result of a demographic explosion, 130 million hectares of forest – 40 per cent of India's total land surface – have been destroyed through overgrazing and timber exploitation. After China, India has the second highest population in the world. If it had not been for a conservation project initiated in 1973 by Indira Gandhi, tigers would long since have disappeared from India. In 1947, the year when the country gained its independence after a century of colonial rule by England, it was estimated that there were 40,000 tigers. Twenty years later, the number had dwindled to about 2,000, and the tiger joined the list of endangered species. In 1972, despite

Opposite: In view of the limited number of tigers remaining in the wild, the only hope for survival is breeding in captivity. But even then, how can animals be reintroduced to the wild if they have not learned to hunt?

SHELTERING TOGETHER

'Thirty years ago,' says Jean-Jacques Annaud, 'the prime minister of Cambodia, Hun Sen, who was actually in favour of animal conservation, one day found himself face to face with a tiger that was menacing him and his cortege. They were about to kill the animal when some American planes flew overhead to bomb the forest. Tiger and humans then took refuge in a small cave, where they waited side by side until the danger had passed, and when it was all clear, they quietly went their separate ways!'

TIME IS A RIVER THAT SWEEPS ME
ALONG, BUT I AM THE RIVER:
IT IS A TIGER THAT DESTROYS ME,
BUT I AM THE TIGER.

JORGE LUIS BORGES

Opposite: The extinction of the tiger does not worry many of Asia's poor, for whom it represents a permanent threat, particularly to their livestock.

a firm decision by the Indian government to ban hunting and trading in the skins, tigers continued to disappear and the number had dropped to 1,800. The WWF (World-Wide Fund for Nature) organized an international campaign to save the tiger and its habitat. Nine reserves were created, and others followed. In these sanctuaries, the Indian government banned all poaching and commercial exploitation of the forests, and imposed limits on the amount of grazing. 4,000 villages were moved to new sites outside these protected areas. Twelve years later, in 1984, the population of tigers had doubled. Sadly, however, this was the year in which Indira Gandhi was assassinated. With her death began a new era in which the protection of the tiger was seen only in terms of the foreign currency that the animal might bring in through tourism.

It is difficult to know just how many tigers remain in the wild, as local representatives run their parks in their own ways. Some will not hesitate to lie about the number of tigers they have, while others close their eyes to the resurgence of poaching. In thirty years, the population of India has increased by 200 million, and the resources of timber and of grass for livestock, which the villagers around the reserves have been able to exploit until now, are rapidly dwindling. The primary consequence of this is that

PEOPLE DO NOT WANT TIGERS IN THEIR OWN BACKYARD.
THE TROUBLE IS, EVERYWHERE IN THE WORLD
IS SOMEBODY'S BACKYARD!

JEAN-JACQUES ANNAUD

the fertile soil and rich vegetation found in the tiger sanctuaries are once more prey to illicit grazing and tree-cutting. The forested corridors that the tigers use to roam from one park to another, thus ensuring a degree of genetic diversity, are now badly affected by this exploitation. Meanwhile, the tigers themselves are being trapped and poisoned for the fat profits to be made out of Chinese contraband. Those that survive in the reserves are deprived of prey, and so they attack humans and livestock. Around Dudhwa National Park, in Uttar Pradesh, 170 people have been killed in the last ten years.

Elsewhere, however, the tiger has been protected without it being at the expense of the human population. A third of the income generated by the Chitwan reserve in Nepal has been used to build schools and dispensaries, and many jobs have been created. At the same time, there has been far less poaching. Fateh Singh Rathore, a leading figure in the preservation of the tiger in India, is acutely aware of the degree to which the fate of humanity and that of the tiger are linked together. In the 50,000 hectares of virgin forest in Ranthambhore Park, where his princely ancestors used to hunt tigers, he has supported the local people for more than thirty years, in return for their help in protecting the tiger. He has opened a hospital, built nurseries, developed a dairy farm, set up a cooperative, and promoted the use of cow dung as a fuel to replace firewood.

A Last Refuge

The Siberian or Amur tiger, a species that once lived in the plains and forests of north-east China, southern Siberia, and the Korean peninsula is now found only in the Amur Valley in Russia, its last refuge. After the Chinese had hunted the tiger almost to extinction, the alarm bell finally sounded in 1962, and the species was officially declared protected. The year 1989 saw the break-up of the Soviet Union and the raising of the Iron Curtain. Firearms were freely available, as were four-wheel drive vehicles, and these factors opened

Opposite: Once the tiger was protected by the animist beliefs of local peoples.

Below: For the genepool of a species to survive without problems caused by close interbreeding, the population must not fall below 500 individuals. This threshold has already been reached almost everywhere.

ATTEMPTS AT REINTRODUCTION

Since the 1970s, wildlife reserves have begun to breed animals with the intention of eventually taking them back to the wild. Rare species that have already been reintroduced include Przewalski's horse, the American wolf, the Arabian oryx, and the Brazilian tamarind monkey. Zoos, however, play a very minor role in conservation, especially for tigers, which are solitary animals. It is almost impossible for a tiger born in captivity to be returned to the wild, simply because it is a predator, and needs to spend 18 to 24 months with its mother, learning to hunt. If an untrained animal were released, even into an area full of prey, it might become a danger both to humans and to their livestock. The Chinese, however, began an experiment in September 2003. Two young tigers from Shanghai Zoo were released into a South African reserve, where human trainers began teaching them to hunt. In a few years, they will be returned to a purpose-built reserve in south China.

WHAT WILL IT SAY ABOUT THE HUMAN RACE IF WE LET THE TIGER GO EXTINCT?

ASHOK KUMAR, VICE-PRESIDENT OF THE WILDLIFE PROTECTION SOCIETY OF INDIA

Opposite: On the borders of Siberia, the Tungus – the last remaining survivors of an ancient people – mourn the passing of their 'brother tiger' and the exploitation of their land, which has put their own survival in jeopardy.

Overleaf: By transforming the environment of this planet, mankind is destroying its biological diversity.

the way to plundering the natural resources of the taiga: coniferous forests, wildlife, minerals. A network of criminal gangs became established, and once again, the tiger found itself at the heart of a vast trade in skins and by-products destined for China.

The Siberian Tiger Project was founded in 1992 at the instigation of a team of Russian and American scientists. The project involved studying the population of Amur tigers by fitting them with collars containing transmitters, so that their movements, reproduction, and way of life under the impact of encroaching civilization could be monitored year by year – all of which would help to protect them more efficiently. The scientists were supported by anti-poaching brigades whose task was to supervise the vast area and to ensure that the 400 surviving tigers could continue to live undisturbed.

What, however, can the future be for an animal that lives in a country where one single specimen can bring in the equivalent of five years' salary for an ordinary worker? How can we feel optimistic in view of the disastrous mismanagement of the

forests (through lack of political will), plus the untrustworthiness of the multinationals from Japan, Korea and America, to whom thousands of hectares of forest land have been ceded, which they are free to cut down as they please? The soil is made barren, there is no replanting, and vast tracts of land are transformed into desert, cutting down the tiger's habitat, decimating its potential prey, and opening the way to the poachers.

Maurice Hornocker, one of the world's leading experts on tigers and co-founder of the Siberian Tiger Project, still believes in the bond between humanity and nature, and is striving to get others to return to their cultural traditions: 'In the past, commerce in sustainable forest products such as berries, nuts, mushrooms, ginseng and wild honey flourished in many communities. We are working with community leaders to revive many of these economically viable cottage industries. Such practices can enhance a forest ecosystem for tigers and their prey while providing for the people.'

The tiger is not the only victim of this destructive exploitation of the taiga. The ancient peoples that have inhabited these forests for centuries have also lost their ancestral lands. The Tungus, among the few people who still regard the tiger as a member of their family, feel that their fate is bound to that of the creature they call 'Amba', and this close kinship will mean that they too are doomed to extinction.

TEST-TUBE TIGERS

When the human population exerts too much pressure on the tiger's habitat, it prevents the genetic regeneration that is necessary for any species to survive. It is well known that interbreeding between family members results in deficiencies of the immune system, infertility, and a higher mortality rate among the young. To alleviate this problem, various methods of assisted reproduction – artificial insemination, *in vitro* fertilization, surrogacy, cloning – have been used since 1998 on tigers in India, at the initiative of the CCMB institute in Hyderabad. The Chinese have recently set up a sperm bank to collect and preserve tiger semen, with a view to ensuring the survival of the species.

EPILOGUE

Is extinction inevitable?

With only about 5,000 tigers now living in the wild, the species really does seem to be under a death sentence. Barring a miracle, there is very little chance that future generations will ever be able to see this magnificent animal in its natural surroundings. This is a sad reflection on the current state of the planet. The imminent disappearance of this great predator is the tragic consequence of a combination of irresponsible human actions – hunting, deforestation, poaching, and illegal trading. It is also a result of the demographic pressure caused by human population growth and by the inability of governments to enforce laws that are designed to

protect animals and their habitat. Just because the Earth has undergone five periods of large-scale extinction, in the course of which nearly all species were wiped out, there are even some people who naively think that the disappearance of the tiger is part of the natural order of things. But they could not be more wrong. The speed at which species of animals and plants are dying out today is, according to experts, between 1,000 and 10,000 times faster than that which marked the geological epochs.

The Earth has never been host to so many different species, and yet paradoxically it has never known such wholesale destruction over so short a period. When an animal such as the tiger, at the top of the food chain, becomes extinct, this leads to the certain death of hundreds of plants and animals, for they are all dependent on one another.

It is depressing to hear that even today, somewhere in the Chinese province of Yunnan, there are still organized fights between tigers, lions and wolves. We can only hope that this book, together with Jean-Jacques Annaud's film, will not only draw attention to the beauty of these animals, but will also increase awareness of our responsibilities as human beings. If the tiger dies, then a part of ourselves will also disappear forever.

BIBLIOGRAPHY

Baikov, Nikolai, *Big Game Hunting in Manchuria*, London, 1936

Bazé, William, *Tiger! Tiger!*, London, 1957

Berg, Bengt, *Tigrar*, Stockholm, 1934

Cheminaud, Guy, *Mes chasses au Laos, les bêtes sauvages de l'Indochine*, Paris, 1939–42

Cyrulnik, Boris, *Mémoires de singes et paroles d'hommes*, Paris, 1983

Cyrulnik, Boris, *Les nourritures affectives*, Paris, 1993

Cyrulnik, Boris, *L'ensorcellement du monde*, Paris, 1997

Cyrulnik, Boris (ed.), *Si les lions pouvaient parler*, Paris, 1998

Dagens, Bruno, *Angkor: Heart of an Asian Empire*, London, 1989

Delaby, Laurence, *Bataclan chamanique raisonné*, Paris, 1997

Hamayon, Roberte, *La chasse à l'âme, esquisse d'une théorie du chamanisme sibérien*, Paris, 1990

Ives, Richard, *Of Tigers & Men: Entering the Age of Extinction*, Edinburgh, 1996

Locke, Arthur, *The Tigers of Trengganu*, London, 1954

Loisel, Gustave, *Histoire des ménageries, de l'antiquité à nos jours*, Paris, 1912

Lorenz, Konrad, *Studies in Animal and Human Behaviour*, London, 1970–71

McDougal, Charles, *The Face of the Tiger*, London, 1977

Matthiessen, Peter, and Hornocker, Maurice, *Tigers in the Snow*, London, 2000

Millet, Fernand, *Les grands animaux sauvages de l'Annam*, Paris, 1930

Montpensier, Ferdinand François, Duke of, *En Indo-Chine: mes chasses, mes voyages*, Paris, 1912

Nowell, Kristin, and Jackson, Peter, *Wild Cats: Status Survey and Conservation Action Plan*, Cambridge, 1996

Perry, Richard, *The World of the Tiger*, London, 1964

Plas, A., *Les grandes chasses en Indochine*, Paris, 1932

Rathore, Fateh Singh, Singh, Tejbir, and Thapar, Valmik, *With Tigers in the Wild: an Experience in an Indian Forest*, New Delhi, 1983

Schaller, George, *The Deer and the Tiger: A Study of Wildlife in India*, Chicago and London, 1967

Seidensticker, John, and Lumpkin, Susan (eds), *Great Cats*, Emmaus, PA, 1991

Speaight, George, *A History of the Circus*, London, 1980

Sunquist, Fiona and Mel, *Tiger Moon*, Chicago, 1988

Thapar, Valmik, *Secret Life of Tigers*, Oxford, 1989

Tilson, Ronald L., *Tigers of the World: The Biology, Biopolitics, Management and Conservation of Endangered Species*, Park Ridge, NJ, 1997

ACKNOWLEDGMENTS

For this wonderful human and animal adventure, the author would like to express her warmest gratitude to the film crew of *Two Brothers*, and especially to Jean-Jacques Annaud, Flore Michiels, Thierry Le Portier, and Xavier Castano for their support and cooperation. Thanks also to Noëlle Boisson, Cyril Oberlechner, Stan Collet, Nicolas Roussiau, Karen Le Portier, Monique Angeon – and, of course, Josette, Kumal, Sangha, Indra Taïga and the rest! The author would also like to thank Isabelle Jendron and Odile Perrard for their trust, their generous help and their invaluable advice. Thanks also to Anne-Marie Bourgeois for her magnificent work and to Nancy Dorking for her sharp eyes. Another big thank you to Boris Cyrulnik.

The publishers are deeply grateful above all to Jean-Jacques Annaud, whose enthusiasm accompanied this project at every stage of its development, and also to the location crew and, in particular, to Flore Michiels for her unfailing commitment. Our heartfelt thanks also to Sherri Aldos and Denis Mignan.

INDEX

CREDITS

Film Credits

PATHÉ presents **TWO BROTHERS**, a film by **JEAN-JACQUES ANNAUD**

with GUY PEARCE, JEAN-CLAUDE DREYFUS, PHILIPPINE LEROY BEAULIEU, FREDDIE HIGHMORE, OANH NGUYEN, MOUSSA MAASKRI, VINCENT SCARITO, MAI ANH LE, JARAN PHETJAREON ('SITAO'), STEPHANIE LAGARDE, ANNOP VARAPANYA ('MU'), BERNARD FLAVIEN, and TEERAWAT MULVILAI, SOMJIN CHIMWONG, NOZHA KHOUADRA, THAVIRAP TANTIWONGSE, BOONSONG BUATONG, DAVID GAN, CAROLINE WILDI, JULIET HOWLAND, JERRY HOH, TONGDEE KAWGAEW, THOMAS LARGET, BO GAULTIER DE KERMOAL, SAID SERRARI, DELPHINE KASSEM, XAVIER CASTANO, CHRISTOPHE CHEYSSON

Tigers trained and directed by THIERRY LE PORTIER
with the assistance of MONIQUE ANGEON

Screenplay ALAIN GODARD & JEAN-JACQUES ANNAUD
Music STEPHEN WARBECK
Produced by JAKE EBERTS, PAUL RASSAM, JEAN-JACQUES ANNAUD
Executive Producer XAVIER CASTANO
Film Editing NOELLE BOISSON
Cinematography JEAN-MARIE DREUJOU, AFC
Production Design PIERRE QUEFFELEAN
Costume Design PIERRE-YVES GAYRAUD
Script Supervisor LAURENCE DUVAL-ANNAUD
Distributed by Pathé Distribution
TWO BROTHERS is a registered trademark of Pathé Renn and Two Brothers
Production Limited, licensed by Universal Studios Licensing LLLP.

Photo Credits

© David Koskas: pp. 1, 4–5, 6–7, 8–9, 10–11, 12, 15, 18–19, 24, 25, 26, 27, 28–29, 30, 31, 32, 33, 38, 39, 40–41, 42–43, 53, 58, 59, 60–61, 67, 71, 82, 83, 84–85, 86–87, 97, 102, 107, 108, 109, 110–111, 112–113, 120–121, 122, 128, 131, 132, 133, 134–135, 136–137, 138, 139, 141, 142, 145, 146–147, 149, 152, 153, 155, 166, 171, 174–175, 178–179, 183
© Jean-Jacques Annaud: pp. 2–3, 118–119, 127, 162, 168–169
© Christophe Cheysson: p. 44
© Bios: pp. 124–125, 173 (Ferrero/Labat)
© Bridgeman Giraudon: pp.47 (private collection), 54 (Stapleton Collection), 63
© Hoa-Qui: pp. 50 (Patrick de Wilde), 73, 116 (True North Images), 158–159 (Franck Lubasseck)
© R.M.N.: pp. 37, 48–49 (P. Bernard)
© Roger-Viollet: pp. 52, 68–69, 95, 157
© Royal Artillery Museum, Woolwich, England: p. 74
© Rue des Archives: p. 64 (below)
Storyboard Fanny Vassou © Pathé Renn Productions: pp. 36, 56, 80, 106, 130, 154
Billy Arjan Singh Collection: p. 176 (second from left)
Panem & Circonstances Collection: pp. 81, 88, 90–91, 92–93, 98, 100–101
Private collections: pp. 65, 70 (*Journal des Voyages*), 76–77, 96 (*Journal des Voyages*), 103, 170 (*Tigrar* by Bengt Berg), 176 (fourth from left), 177 (second, third and fourth from left)
Photothèque Hachette: pp. 64 (above), 66, 115 (National Museum of Korea, Seoul), 123, 148, 151, 164–165 (Musée de la Chasse et de la Nature, Paris).
Vérascopes Richard: pp. 79, 126, 176 (first from left), 177 (first from left)
Animals selected by Jim Harter: pp. 22–23, 34–35, 104–105, 140.

Translated from the French *Tigres* by David H. Wilson

First published in hardback in the United Kingdom in 2004
by Thames & Hudson Ltd, 181A High Holborn, London WC1V 7QX
www.thamesandhudson.com

First published in 2004 in hardcover in the United States of America
by Thames & Hudson Inc., 500 Fifth Avenue, New York, New York 10110
thamesandhudsonusa.com

ISBN 0-500-51193-4
Library of Congress Catalogue Card Number: 2004104539

British Library Cataloguing-in-Publication Data
A catalogue record for this book is available from the British Library

Printed in France - L93400

the Media

Central to the plot of Spiceworld are the mischievous attempts by tabloid newspaper editor, Kevin McMaxford (played by Barry Humphries), to ruin the Spice Girls' careers. McMaxford is sick of good news about the Spice Girls. He wants a new kind of Spice splash – bad news.

Tuesday, 10 June

Once again we're shooting at the big manor house in Guildford. (I'd love to live there.)

We're being plagued by the press. Some of them were so desperate to get a scoop that they disguised themselves as a panto horse. They even tried to fake a story by getting a security guard in a scuffle.

During a visit from their heavily-pregnant friend Nicola, the Spice Girls imagine the day when they too will be mothers.

McMaxford puts Damien, a paparazzi photographer (played by Richard O'Brien) on the case. Damien is a photographer version of an SAS undercover counter-surveillance expert. Under his coat, half a dozen cameras clink together. Damien follows the Girls around trying to pick up negative newsworthy nuggets. At one point he pops out of a toilet in the middle of the night at the house where they're staying. Sensing the intrusion, they all wake up and run into each other's rooms. Later Damien overhears them discussing their imminent live concert.

McMaxford: I want their dreams shattered, Brad. I want the ground to crack and a huge yawning chasm to open up beneath them. I want them destroyed.

Another crack of thunder, then rain starts falling.

McMaxford: Who's going to help me, Brad? Who's going to help me take on Girl Power and bring it crashing to the ground?

Wednesday, 11 June

BATTERSEA PARK SET-UP.

Our first scene was a flash-forward to our futures – as mothers – which was absolutely hilarious. We all looked wicked. Mel B was dressed up like an African mama, Emma looked the perfect wife – butter wouldn't melt in her mouth, Victoria was a drunken Joan Collins, Mel C was Waynetta in a fat suit and I was just a glamorous Hilda. The Dream Boys came down with their fake tans – ugh! – and there were paparazzi waiting in the trees.

It's quite funny how we're driven such a short distance from our winnebago to the set, so that the paparazzi hiding in the bushes don't snap us!

Today we shot the bedroom scene. It was quite hilarious pretending to be really scared. Creeping down the corridor and bumping into one another was very funny. I was tripping over my Babs Windsor nightie and trying not to laugh at Mel B – oh, and trying not to stare straight into camera! A good day and not too long.